PART
ONE

THE UNITED NATIONS ORGANISATION

'The Solidarity of Peoples' – *the painted ceiling of the League of Nations Council Room in the Palace of Nations at Geneva. Only a year after this symbol of international co-operation was completed in 1938, the Second World War began*

Around 5,000 million people live on this planet. All are members of a single, human race, but they are divided in every imaginable way. They speak 4,500 languages. They have an amazing variety of religious beliefs, societies and cultures. They live in 168 separate countries, each with its own kind of government and law. And for thousands of years they have fought each other in countless wars. For most of their history, humans have been a divided, warring race.

Despite this, during the last fifty years, there has been a rapid growth of organisations which join people and their countries together. Some have a world-wide membership, such as the United Nations Organisation. Others, like the European Community or the Organisation of African States, have a regional membership. Such organisations aim to achieve co-operation, peace and security between their member states. By 1990 around 500 international organisations were in active existence.

Why have so many international organisations come into being in the twentieth century? What do countries hope to achieve by joining them? How well do they serve their purposes? This book aims to answer these questions by examining two important examples – the United Nations Organisation and the European Community.

1

1

ORIGINS OF THE UNITED NATIONS

The history of the United Nations begins with a top secret wartime meeting on board a ship in the Atlantic Ocean in 1941.

The Atlantic Charter

The meeting was between Winston Churchill, Prime Minister of Great Britain, and Franklin Roosevelt, President of the United States. They met on the warship *HMS Prince of Wales* off the coast of Newfoundland in the Atlantic Ocean, from 9–12 August 1941.

Britain at that time was at war with Germany and Italy, which were known as the 'Axis Powers'. The United States, though not at war, was giving aid to help Britain fight them. The purpose of the meeting between Churchill and Roosevelt was to discuss the future of the world at the end of the war. The result was a declaration by the two leaders called **The Atlantic Charter.**

The Atlantic Charter outlined eight 'hopes for a better future of the world'. Chief amongst these were the hopes that all countries would have democratic governments, that countries would trade freely with each other and share in economic prosperity, and that countries would reduce their weapons. To help achieve such aims, there would be 'a wider and permanent system of general security'.

The United Nations Declaration

Only four months after the Atlantic Charter was signed, the United States went to war with Japan, which had joined Germany and Italy as one of the Axis Powers. This meant that the USA was now a partner in war of Britain and all Britain's allies. Roosevelt suggested that all the states now at war against the Axis Powers should be called The United Nations.

Roosevelt's suggestion was accepted. On 1 January 1942, twenty-six governments who were at war against the Axis signed a **United Nations Declaration,** stating that they agreed with the hopes and ideas of the Atlantic Charter. Although the twenty-six nations were meant to be equal, the Declaration was signed first by the four most powerful – the United States, Britain, the Soviet Union and China.

Wartime Conferences

Over the next three years, the 'Big Four' members of the United Nations held meetings to discuss how they would put the Atlantic Charter into effect. At a conference in Moscow in October 1943, the Big Four drew up the **Moscow Declaration,** stating that they would set up a 'General International Organisation' as soon as possible. Its job would be to maintain world peace and security. All peace-loving nations could become members.

The most important of their meetings took place at Dumbarton Oaks, a suburb of Washington, capital of the USA, in 1944. At the **Dumbarton Oaks Conference,** diplomats from the Big Four countries drew up a set of detailed plans for the 'General International Organisation'. The chief proposal was that:

A 'There should be established an international organisation under the title of the United Nations . . . .
  The purposes of the organisation should be:
  1. To maintain international peace and security . . .
  2. To develop friendly relations among nations . . .
  3. . . . the solution of international economic, social and other humanitarian problems.
  4. To afford a centre for harmonising the actions of nations in the achievement of these common ends . . . '

Early in 1945 Churchill and Roosevelt met the Soviet leader, Stalin, at Yalta in the USSR. At the **Yalta Conference** they agreed on the voting arrangements that would be used for making decisions in the new organisation. In general, each nation would have one vote in a United Nations Assembly. There were, however, some important exceptions. The USSR would have three votes because two republics of the Soviet Union, Byelorussia and the Ukraine, would have their own seats in the Assembly. Self-governing dominions of the British Empire, such as Canada and Australia, would also have a vote each, even though they were not independent nations. And, most important, each of the Big Four would have the **right of veto** over certain decisions. This meant that a decision could only be made if all the Big Four agreed to it; if one disagreed, it could not be put into effect.

The San Francisco Conference

On 25 April 1945, as the Second World War was coming to an end, delegates from fifty of the United Nations met in San Francisco in the USA for the last of the wartime UN conferences.

2

Harry S. Truman, who became US President after the death of Roosevelt on 12 April, said to the opening session of the San Francisco conference:

B 'At no time in history has there been a more important conference or a more necessary meeting than this one . . .

You members of this conference are to be architects of the better world. In your hands rests our future . . .

We who have lived through the torture and the strategy of two world conflicts must realise the magnitude of the problem before us. We do not need far-sighted vision to understand the trend in recent history . . . With ever-increasing brutality and destruction, modern warfare, if unchecked, would ultimately crush all civilisation. We still have a choice between the alternatives – the continuation of international chaos or the establishment of a world organisation for the enforcement of peace. . .

This conference will devote its energies and its labours exclusively to the single problem of setting up the essential organisation to keep the peace. You are to write the fundamental charter.'

It took the delegates at San Francisco two months to hammer out the details of the **Charter**, or set of rules, of the United Nations Organisation. When they had finished, they met in the San Francisco Opera House to sign it, solemnly and in turn. On that day, 25 June 1945, the United Nations Organisation, commonly called the UN, thus came into being.

Delegates from China sign the Charter of the United Nations in San Francisco's Opera House on 26 June 1945

Work section

A.
1. Make a time line starting in August 1941 and ending in June 1945.
2. Mark onto it seven events which led to the creation of the United Nations in 1945. Write a sentence after each one briefly describing what happened.
3. What evidence is there in your completed time line that the UN was the idea and creation of Britain, the USA and the USSR?

B. Study the photograph above, then answer these questions:
1. Decribe the symbol of the United Nations hanging at the back of the stage. Suggest what it was meant to symbolise.
2. What purposes do you think this ceremony was meant to serve?

C. In source B, Harry Truman spoke of the 'magnitude of the problem before us'. Under headings 1–4 in source A, list the problems likely to arise in putting those four aims into practice.

2

STRUCTURE OF THE UNITED NATIONS

The Charter drawn up at the San Francisco Conference consisted of 111 articles, describing the purposes of the UN and explaining how it would do its work.

Sources A–G below are extracts from the Charter, showing how it created six organs to do the work of the UN. As you read each one, you should do exercise A, which is linked to it, on page 5.

A   Article 7
There are established as the principal organs of the United Nations: a General Assembly, a Security Council, an Economic and Social Council, a Trusteeship Council, an International Court of Justice and a Secretariat.

B   Articles 9–20: The General Assembly
9 The General Assembly shall consist of all the Members of the United Nations.
11 The General Assembly may consider the general principles of international peace and security, including the principles governing disarmament. . . [It] may discuss any questions relating to the maintenance of international peace and security . . . and may make recommendations with regard to any such questions . . .
13 The General Assembly shall . . . make recommendations for the purpose of:
a. promoting international co-operation in the political field and encouraging the development of international law. . .
b. promoting international co-operation in the economic, social, cultural, educational and health fields, and assisting in the realisation of human rights and fundamental freedoms for all.
18 Each member of the General Assembly shall have one vote. Decisions shall be by a two-thirds majority.
20 The General Assembly shall meet in regular annual sessions and in such special sessions as occasion might require.

C   Articles 23–43: The Security Council
23 The Security Council shall consist of eleven members of the United Nations. China, France, the Union of Soviet Socialist Republics, the United Kingdom and the United States of America shall be permanent members. The General Assembly shall elect six other members to be non-permanent members.
24 In order to ensure prompt and effective action by the United Nations, its members confer on the Security Council primary responsibility for the maintenance of international peace and security.
27 Each member of the Security Council shall have one vote. Decisions . . . shall be made by an affirmative vote of seven members including the concurring votes of the permanent members.
34 The Security Council may investigate any dispute or

any situation which might lead to international friction or give rise to a dispute. . .
41 The Security Council may decide what measures not involving the use of armed force are to be employed to give effect to its decisions. . . These may include complete or partial interruption of economic relations and of rail, sea, air, postal, telegraphic, radio and other means of communication, and the severance of diplomatic relations.
42 Should the Security Council consider that measures provided for in Article 41 would be inadequate . . . it may take such action by air, sea or land forces as may be necessary to restore international peace and security. Such action may include demonstrations, blockade, and other operations by air, sea or land forces of Members of the United Nations.

D   Articles 55–67: The Economic and Social Council
55 . . . the United Nations shall promote:
a. higher standards of living, full employment, and conditions of economic and social progress and development;
b. solutions of international economic, social, health and related problems, and international cultural and educational cooperation; and
c. universal respect for, and observance of, human rights and fundamental freedoms for all without distinction as to race, sex, language or religion.
57 The various specialised agencies having wide international responsibilities . . . in economic, social, cultural, educational, health and related fields shall be brought into relationship with the United Nations. Such agencies are hereinafter referred to as specialised agencies.
61 The Economic and Social Council shall consist of twenty-seven Members of the United Nations elected by the General Assembly. . .
62 The Council may make studies or reports with respect to international economic, social, cultural, educational, health and related and matters and may make recommendations with respect to any such matters. . .
63 The Council may enter into agreements with any of the agencies referred to in Article 57. It may co-ordinate the activities of the specialised agencies.
67 Each member of the Council shall have one vote.

E   Articles 73–86: The Trusteeship Council
73 Members of the United Nations which have responsibilities for territories whose peoples have not yet attained self-government recognise that the interests of the inhabitants of these territories are paramount, and accept as a sacred trust to promote the well-being of the inhabitants.
75 The United Nations shall establish under its authority an international trusteeship system for the administration and supervision of such territories. . . These territories are hereinafter referred to as trust territories.
76 The basic objectives of the trusteeship system shall be . . . to promote the political, economic, social and edu-

4

cational advancement of the inhabitants of the trust territories, and their progressive development towards self-government or independence.
89 Each member of the Council shall have one vote . . . Decisions shall be made by a majority of members voting.

F   Articles 92–98: The International Court of Justice
92 The International Court of Justice shall be the principal judicial organ of the United Nations.
93 All Members of the United Nations are parties to the International Court of Justice.
94 Each member of the United Nations undertakes to

comply with the decision of the court in any case to which it is a party.
[Other rules of the ICJ are contained in a separate Statute, eg. no. 3, The Court shall consist of fifteen members, no two of whom may be nationals of the same state.]

G   Articles 98–101: the Secretariat
The Secretariat shall comprise a Secretary-General and such staff as the Organisation may require. The Secretary-General shall be appointed by the General Assembly upon the recommendation of the Security Council. He shall be the chief administrative officer.

The UN Headquarters in New York, photographed from a plane flying above the East River, nears completion in June 1952

Work section

A. 1. On a full page, make a grid like the one below. Then, using source A for information, put the names of the six 'principal organs' into the first column.

Principal organs of the UN

Name	Membership	Purposes	How it makes decisions

2. Taking information from source B, briefly note the General Assembly's membership, purposes and way of making decisions in columns 2–4 of your grid.

3. Using sources C–G for information, do the same for the other principal organs, until your grid is filled with brief notes.

B. Refer to column 3 of your completed grid. Describe in your own words the main purposes of the UN.

C. Read articles 41–42 in source C again. Explain in your own words how the Security Council could deal with threats to international peace.

D. List the kinds of secretarial and clerical staff you think were needed in the UN Secretariat. How does this help to explain the size of the Secretariat building in the photograph above?

3

THE UN AS PEACEKEEPER, 1945–49

The UN spent six months organising itself to do its work. The first General Assembly met in London in January 1946 and elected members to the principal organs. The most important of these, the Security Council, then appointed Trygve Lie of Norway as Secretary-General of the UN.

These were easy tasks. Almost at once, however, the UN was asked to deal with more difficult business – a series of crises which threatened world peace.

Crisis in Iran and the Balkans

The first crisis was brought to the UN by Iran in January 1946. Iran complained that Soviet troops, still present after being stationed there during World War Two, were meddling in Iran's internal affairs. It asked the Security Council to halt this interference.

This first test of the UN as a peacekeeper looked straightforward. However, the situation was complicated by the fact that two of its leading members, the USA and the USSR, were now on bad terms. Since the end of World War Two the two countries had come to mistrust each other. A state of **Cold War** now

existed between them, meaning that they used every method of opposing each other short of open warfare.

When Iran took its complaint to the UN, the Soviets thought it had been encouraged to do so by the USA and its main ally, Britain. They saw the complaint as a 'Cold War' tactic being used by the USA. The Soviets responded by claiming that Britain too was meddling in another country's affairs – Greece, where British troops were helping the Greek government fight communist rebels.

The British and Americans in the UN Security Council were angered by this accusation. They claimed that the British troops in Greece had been invited there by the Greek government. Angry debates took place in the Council.

The Council decided not to investigate the Soviet complaint against Britain, but it did investigate Greek complaints that Yugoslavia, Bulgaria and Albania were helping the Greek rebels to fight the Greek government (see map). A Special Committee on the Balkans (UNSCOB) was set up, however, to deal with the matter. This too failed to halt the fighting which only came to an end when Yugoslavia stopped giving arms to the rebels in 1948.

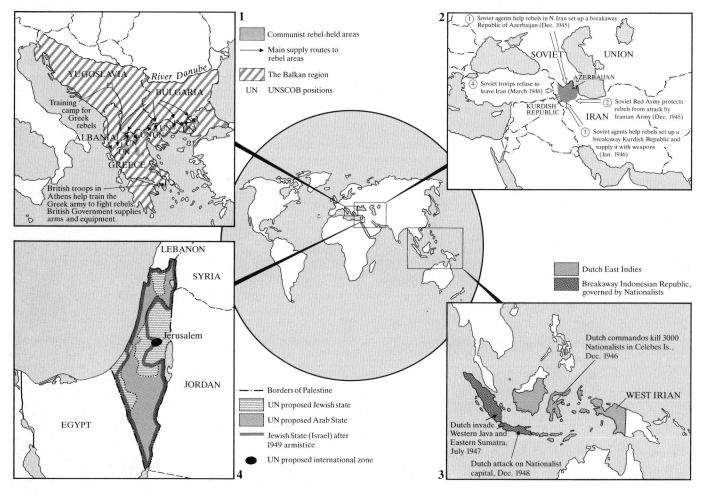

1
- Communist rebel-held areas
- → Main supply routes to rebel areas
- The Balkan region
- UN UNSCOB positions

YUGOSLAVIA · River Danube · BULGARIA · Training camp for Greek rebels · ALBANIA · GREECE

British troops in Athens help train the Greek army to fight rebels. British Government supplies arms and equipment.

2
① Soviet agents help rebels in N. Iran set up a breakaway Republic of Azerbaijan (Dec. 1945)

SOVIET UNION · AZERBAIJAN

④ Soviet troops refuse to leave Iran (March 1946)

KURDISH REPUBLIC · IRAN

② Soviet Red Army protects rebels from attack by Iranian Army (Dec. 1945)

③ Soviet agents help rebels set up a breakaway Kurdish Republic and supply it with weapons (Jan. 1946)

LEBANON · SYRIA · Jerusalem · JORDAN · EGYPT

- – – Borders of Palestine
- UN proposed Jewish state
- UN proposed Arab State
- Jewish State (Israel) after 1949 armistice
- ● UN proposed international zone

4

- Dutch East Indies
- Breakaway Indonesian Republic, governed by Nationalists

Dutch commandos kill 3000 Nationalists in Celebes Is., Dec. 1946

WEST IRIAN

Dutch invade Western Java and Eastern Sumatra, July 1947

Dutch attack on Nationalist capital, Dec. 1948

3

In Iran, meanwhile, the Iranian government opened talks with the Soviets. Without any UN involvement, it persuaded them to withdraw their troops in May 1946.

Crisis in Indonesia

The next problem brought before the UN concerned Indonesia, a Dutch colony in South-East Asia.

The problem arose in 1945 when Indonesian nationalists declared the colony an independent republic. The Dutch reacted by sending troops to fight the nationalists in what it called a 'police action'. The UN protested, but the Dutch claimed it was a domestic matter and no business of the UN.

After a particularly brutal 'police action' in 1947, the UN Security Council ordered a cease-fire between the Dutch and the nationalists. Both sides obeyed. To try to settle the dispute, the UN set up a 'Good Offices Committee' which persuaded the two sides to agree to share the government of Indonesia.

The agreement lasted for a year until the Dutch attacked the nationalists in another violent 'police action'. The Security Council again stepped in, calling for full independence for Indonesia. The Dutch rejected the UN's call, but quickly changed their mind when the US threatened to cut off 400 million dollars worth of aid to their country. After lengthy talks the two sides made peace, and the Dutch gave Indonesia independence in December 1949.

'Before the glue has time to set'. An American cartoon of 1946 commenting on a lack of cohesion in the UN

Crisis in Palestine

The UN's most difficult test began in 1947 when Britain asked it to consider the future of Palestine in the Middle East.

Britain had governed Palestine on behalf of the League of Nations, fore-runner of the UN, since 1920. During that time, Palestinian Arabs had often clashed with Jewish immigrants settling in large numbers in the country. The British army, trying to keep order, came under attack from both Palestinians and Jews. By 1947, having failed to keep order, Britain asked the UN to take on the job of keeping peace in Palestine.

The General Assembly's first action was to form a UN Special Committee on Palestine (UNSCOP). This eleven-man team visited the Middle East and drew up a plan to divide Palestine into a Jewish state and an Arab state. Although the Arab countries around Palestine made it clear that they would not accept the proposed Jewish state, the General Assembly approved this partition plan in November 1947.

UNSCOP's partition plan came to nothing. As soon as the British left Palestine in May 1948 the Jews set up the state of Israel in the areas given to them by the plan. The surrounding Arab states immediately invaded Israel, trying to destroy the new state.

The UN now had a full-scale war to deal with. The Security Council sent a team to mediate between the two sides. Led by the Swedish Count Bernadotte, the mediators quickly arranged a four-week truce. As soon as the truce ended, however, fighting started again. A further blow to the UN mediators came in September when Bernadotte was murdered in Jerusalem.

Bernadotte's successor, Ralph Bunche, managed to organise another truce in 1949. Under his guidance, armistice agreements were signed between Israel and all but one of the Arab states. However, this was only a truce. No peace treaty was signed, and the Arabs continued to attack Israel by other means, such as closing the Suez Canal to Israeli ships. As we shall see, the truce was a fragile one; three more wars took place between Israel and the Arab states in the coming years.

THE UN AND THE KOREAN WAR

At three o'clock in the morning of 25 June 1950, UN Secretary-General Trygve Lie was woken from bed by a telephone call. His caller, a United States representative at the UN, told him that the army of North Korea had invaded South Korea. The US government, he told Lie, wanted the matter brought immediately before the Security Council.

Background to the invasion

From 1910 to 1945, Korea was part of Japan. When the Allies defeated Japan in World War Two in 1945, US and Soviet forces moved into Korea. Soviet troops occupied the country north of the 38th Parallel (*line of latitude*) while American troops occupied Korea south of the 38th Parallel.

In 1947 the UN declared that elections should be held in both parts of Korea to choose a government for the whole country. It set up a UN Commission to observe the elections to make sure they were fair.

In 1948 South Korean voters elected a parliament which then set up a government of the Republic of Korea. The UN Commission observed the election and declared it fair. In northern Korea, however, the Soviets did not allow the UN Commission to observe the elections. So, when communists set up a People's Republic of Korea in the North, the UN said that only the South Korean government was lawful, since it was the only one that had been elected fairly.

Both governments claimed authority over the whole country and started to quarrel. Their troops clashed in battles near the 38th Parallel several times in 1948–50. Meanwhile, Soviet and US troops were withdrawn from the country.

Although the USA and USSR withdrew their forces, they continued to give money and weapons to the Koreans – the USA to the South and the USSR to the Communist North. This meant both were indirectly involved in the conflict between North and South when it began on 25 June 1950.

The UN takes action

Trygve Lie acted fast to deal with the invasion of South Korea. Within twelve hours of his night-time phone call he had arranged an emergency session of the Security Council.

As you read in Chapter 2, there were five permanent and six non-permanent members of the Security Council. Decisions needed a 'yes' vote by seven members, including all the permanent members. Any one of the permanent members could thus **veto** any decision by voting against it.

This last point was crucial on 25 June, for the Soviet member of the Security Council did not attend the meeting that day. The Soviet Union was boycotting (*refusing to attend*) the Council to show that they disliked China being represented on it by the Chinese Nationalist government in Taiwan and not by the Chinese Communist government in Beijing.

At the meeting, the United States claimed that the North Koreans had breached world peace and called on them to withdraw to the 38th Parallel. Nine of the eleven members voted for this resolution and one abstained. But the Soviet member, who would have vetoed it, was not there due to the Soviet boycott.

Two days later the Security Council was told that the North Koreans were ignoring its resolution. The USA therefore drew up a stronger resolution, saying that the UN would help South Korea repel the attack by any means necessary. Again, the Council voted in favour of the resolution because the Soviet member was still boycotting its meetings. Without further discussion, the USA sent forces to South Korea.

1 North Korea invades South Korea June–Sept. 1950

2 UN forces move North, Sept.–October 1950

3 The Chinese offensive, Nov. 1950–Jan. 1951

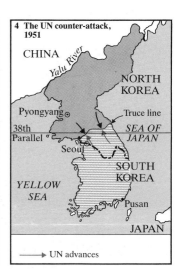

4 The UN counter-attack, 1951

By mid-July the Council had worked out the details of how it would help South Korea. Military forces from sixteen member states would be joined together in a UN Joint Command to fight with the South Korean army against the invaders from the North.

It looked, on the face of it, as if the UN was taking tough action to protect one of its members from attack. In fact, it was a US rather than a UN operation. The USA provided 302,483 of the 341,628 UN troops, 86 per cent of the naval power and 93 per cent of the air power. And an American general, Douglas MacArthur, was its Commander.

The Korean War, 1950–53

As map 1 shows, the North Korean advance was very rapid. Within two months the Communists had bottled up the South Korean and UN troops in a small area around Pusan. Their defeat looked certain.

On 15 September, however, UN troops made a daring sea-borne landing at Inchon and re-took the South Korean capital, Seoul. Now the South Korean and UN troops were able to break out of the Pusan area and drive the Communists back to North Korea.

Despite a warning from China not to cross the 38th Parallel into North Korea, MacArthur's troops continued to advance. By late October they were within 100 km of the Chinese border. As a result, 300,000 Chinese troops moved into North Korea to support the North Korean army. From November to January 1951 they drove back the UN troops, re-took Seoul and advanced into South Korea (see map 3).

UN forces halted the Communists in late January, then gradually pushed them back, crossing the 38th Parallel again on 31 March 1951. MacArthur wanted to continue north and attack China directly, using nuclear weapons to destroy Chinese cities. However, US President Truman feared that this could lead to a world war, and sacked MacArthur.

The war now settled into a stalemate. The two sides built trenches and fortifications on either side of the 38th Parallel, making sure that neither could advance any further. Meanwhile, peace talks began in June 1951, eventually resulting in an armistice signed at **Panmunjom** in July 1953.

Results of the war

The Panmunjom armistice left Korea divided at the

A South Korean street in July 1950, shortly after the UN announced it would help South Korea repel the North Korean invasion.

38th Parallel into two hostile countries. For both North and South Korea, the war had brought appalling destruction. Huge areas lay wrecked and useless. Millions of people were homeless and starving. Some 1.5 million South Koreans and 3.5 million North Koreans were dead.

For the UN the Korean War had serious consequences. While it gained respect by taking prompt action against an aggressor, several developments weakened it. First, the Soviets stopped boycotting the Security Council in August 1950 and started to use their veto to block decisions. To overcome this, the USA put forward a resolution called 'Uniting for Peace'. This said that the Assembly could take over the Security Council's peace-keeping functions if the Security Council was unable to act because a decision was vetoed. However, there were bitter arguments about whether the resolution was legal. For years to come the Soviets and several other members refused to follow decisions made on that basis.

A second consequence of the war was the resignation of Trygve Lie. The Soviets were infuriated by his quick and eager support for UN intervention in Korea, saying it was beyond the scope of his office. The Soviet delegation therefore refused to have any dealings with him, making his position so difficult that he had to resign in 1953.

Finally the war showed, if it wasn't already obvious, that the UN was dominated by the USA, which was using it to further its struggle against the spread of Communism.

Work section

A. Study the photograph above, then answer these questions:
  1. How might a supporter of the UN in 1950 have explained the third line of the banner?
  2. Why might a critic of the UN have said that the banner was incorrect?
  3. Suggest what kind of people put up the banner and what they hoped to achieve by it.

B. 1. Explain the meaning of the term veto.
  2. Why would you expect the Soviet member of the Security Council to veto the decision to send UN troops to Korea? Why did he not veto the decision?
  3. How might the Soviet member's presence in the Security Council on 25 and 27 June 1950 have changed the course of the Korean War?

9

5

THE UN IN THE MIDDLE EAST, 1945–67

You read in Chapter 3 that the UN got involved in Middle Eastern affairs in 1947. It drew up a plan to make British-run Palestine independent and to split it into an Arab state and a Jewish state. However, war broke out between the Jewish state and five nearby Arab countries as soon as the two states were created in 1948. The UN tried to mediate in this war in an attempt to bring peace to the region.

The Armistice and after

As you know, UN mediator Ralph Bunche helped make an armistice agreement between Israel and four of the Arab states – Egypt, Syria, Jordan and Lebanon. This ended the fighting, but it was not a peace treaty. Two big problems had to be solved before a lasting peace could be made.

First, 800,000 Palestinian Arabs had fled from Palestine during the war. They were now living as refugees in camps outside the borders of Israel, as Palestine was now called. These refugees urgently needed re-housing or re-patriation.

Second, the borders between Israel and the neighbouring Arab states were no longer clear. During the war, Israel had grown in size by taking much of the land which the UN gave to the Arabs of Palestine.

The Arab states refused to recognise the borders of this enlarged Israel. Any peace treaty would have to fix borders acceptable to both Arabs and Israelis if the peace was to last.

To deal with these problems the UN set up a Conciliation Commission for Palestine (CCP). The CCP held talks between Israel and the Arab states in neutral Switzerland in 1949–51. It also set up a **UN Relief and Welfare Agency (UNRWA)** to help the Palestinian refugees in their crowded, unhealthy camps.

Sadly, the CCP achieved nothing. At the talks in Switzerland, the Arabs insisted on negotiating with Israel as a single group, while the Israelis insisted on dealing with each country separately. The CCP could not persuade either side to drop its demands, and in 1951 broke off the talks.

Meanwhile, in the refugee camps, young men known as Fedayeen (Arabic for 'self-sacrificer') formed commando groups to make cross-border attacks on Israel. From 1949 to 1955 the Fedayeen killed or wounded some 250 Israelis. In retaliation, the Israeli army made raids against the camps from which the Fedayeen came. As the raids and counter-raids grew more frequent and more violent, the chances of a peace settlement between Arabs and Israelis grew remote.

One of the first UNRWA refugee camps, near Tripoli in Lebanon, photographed in 1952

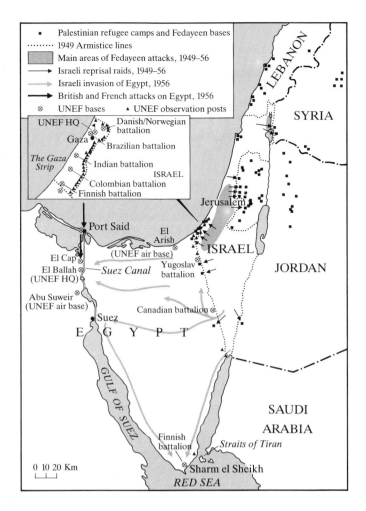

The map legend reads:

- ■ Palestinian refugee camps and Fedayeen bases
- ···· 1949 Armistice lines
- ▨ Main areas of Fedayeen attacks, 1949–56
- → Israeli reprisal raids, 1949–56
- ⇒ Israeli invasion of Egypt, 1956
- ➡ British and French attacks on Egypt, 1956
- ⊗ UNEF bases ▲ UNEF observation posts

UNEF HQ — Danish/Norwegian battalion
Gaza — Brazilian battalion
The Gaza Strip — Indian battalion
ISRAEL
Colombian battalion
Finnish battalion
Jerusalem

Port Said
El Arish (UNEF air base)
El Cap
El Ballah (UNEF HQ) — Suez Canal — Yugoslav battalion
ISRAEL
JORDAN
Abu Suweir (UNEF air base)
Suez
Canadian battalion
E G Y P T
LEBANON
SYRIA
GULF OF SUEZ
SAUDI ARABIA
Finnish battalion — Straits of Tiran
0 10 20 Km
Sharm el Sheikh
RED SEA

The UN and the Suez Crisis, 1956

At the end of October 1956, full-scale war broke out again when the Israeli army invaded Egypt, thus breaking the armistice.

The UN Security Council met immediately to discuss a resolution demanding the withdrawal of Israeli forces. However, unknown to the Council, Israel was not acting alone. Two of the Council's permanent members, France and Britain, had helped the Israelis plan their attack on Egypt. They did so because they were angered by Egypt's nationalisation of the Suez Canal, which was owned by British and French shareholders. Britain and France intended to occupy the Suez Canal zone while the Israelis occupied the area of Egypt east of Suez. So when the Security Council voted on the resolution demanding Israel's

withdrawal, Britain and France vetoed it.

With two of its members on the verge of invading another country, the Security Council used the 'Uniting for Peace' method of overcoming their veto (see page 9). This allowed the Security Council to transfer the handling of the crisis to the General Assembly, where no country had a veto.

The General Assembly met in emergency session on 1 November and called for a ceasefire and the withdrawal of troops. On 4 November it agreed to set up a **United Nations Emergency Force (UNEF)**. The tasks of this multi-nation army group would be to supervise the ceasefire, to arrange the withdrawal of forces, and to keep the peace by putting itself between the Israelis and Egyptians as they withdrew.

The crisis deepened on 5 November when British and French troops parachuted into the Suez Canal zone. There was nothing the UN could do to halt this invasion. However, the US government opposed the British and French action, and threatened to cut off their oil supplies from America. With the Suez Canal, Europe's direct oil route from the Middle East oil fields, now closed to shipping, Britain and France faced oil starvation. They had no choice but to withdraw their troops from Suez.

UNEF in Egypt

The UN Emergency Force began arriving in Egypt on 15 November 1956. By that time the Israelis had gained what they wanted in the war, had stopped their invasion and agreed to a ceasefire. Six thousand UNEF troops were therefore able to position themselves between the Israeli and Egyptian armies.

Wearing light blue helmets and UN armbands, but keeping their national uniforms, the UNEF soldiers were lightly armed with rifles, sub-machine guns, anti-tank rockets and armoured cars. Their orders were to use these weapons only in self-defence and as a last resort. Their purpose was not to fight either of the two sides but to be a buffer between them in case one should attack the other.

UNEF remained in Egypt patrolling the ceasefire line for the next ten years. Being a buffer force was sometimes dangerous, and eighty-nine UNEF soldiers were killed in shooting incidents that flared up from time to time. Nor was the operation cheap, for it cost the UN $213 million to keep UNEF there.

Work section

A. *Armistice: an agreement between enemies to suspend fighting in order to discuss peace.*
Peace treaty: a binding agreement or contract between countries, defining the terms and conditions on which they will live in peace with each other.

   1. What are the differences between an armistice and a peace treaty?
   2. Why could Israel and the Arab states make an armistice agreement in 1949 but not a peace treaty?
   3. Make a list of at least three issues which prevented the making of a peace treaty between the two sides. Which of those issues seemed most difficult to overcome?

B. Study the photograph opposite, then answer these questions:
   1. What was UNRWA and what was it set up to do?
   2. Using the photograph as evidence, describe in detail the problems facing UNWRA.

THE UN IN THE CONGO, 1960–64

The largest and most controversial UN peace-keeping action took place in the Congolese Republic, now called Zaire, between 1960 and 1964.

Chaos in the Congo

Until 1960 the Congo was a Belgian colony. In that year the Belgians announced that they would give it independence.

Although the economy of the Belgian Congo had grown rapidly during the 1950s, it was still a poor country. A development plan written in 1950 said that thirty years were needed to prepare for independence. The Belgian government ignored this, however, and gave the Congolese just five months to prepare for running their own affairs.

The independent Congolese Republic came into being on 30 June 1960, led by Patrice Lumumba as Prime Minister and Joseph Kasavubu as President. Within a week Congolese soldiers in the capital, Leopoldville, mutinied against their white officers. The mutiny was followed by violent attacks on Europeans, especially Belgians.

The mutiny had two effects. First, it took away all power and authority from the week-old government. Second, it caused such terror among the 100,000 Belgians in the Congo that the Belgian government sent paratroopers to protect them. This was illegal, for they were not invited by the new Congolese government.

As chaos spread from the capital, the government was hit by a third crisis. Moise Tshombe, leader of Katanga province in southern Congo, declared Katanga an independent state led by himself. Katanga was mineral-rich, producing 8 per cent of the world's copper, 60 per cent of its uranium and 80 per cent of its industrial diamonds. Backed by the European companies which mined these minerals, Tshombe intended to keep the profits for Katanga.

The UN intervenes

Faced with mutiny in the army, invasion by Belgians, and the breakaway of Katanga, Prime Minister Lumumba appealed for help to the United Nations. At the suggestion of Dag Hammarskjöld, Secretary-General since 1953, the Security Council created a UN army to restore order in the Congo. Known by their French name as ONUC (*Force de l'Organisation des Nations Unies au Congo*), nearly 10,000 UN troops arrived in the Congo during the following two weeks.

ONUC was given four tasks: to restore order and maintain it; to stop other countries involving themselves in the Congo's affairs; to help build the country's economy; and to restore political stability.

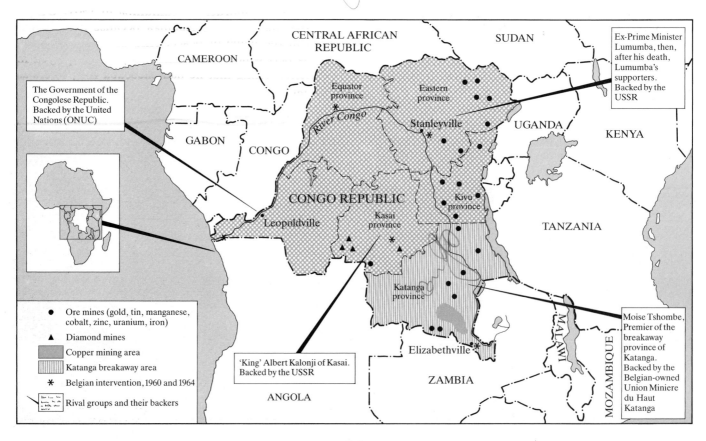

The Government of the Congolese Republic. Backed by the United Nations (ONUC)

Ex-Prime Minister Lumumba, then, after his death, Lumumba's supporters. Backed by the USSR

Moise Tshombe, Premier of the breakaway province of Katanga. Backed by the Belgian-owned Union Miniere du Haut Katanga

'King' Albert Kalonji of Kasai. Backed by the USSR

- ● Ore mines (gold, tin, manganese, cobalt, zinc, uranium, iron)
- ▲ Diamond mines
-   Copper mining area
-   Katanga breakaway area
- ＊ Belgian intervention, 1960 and 1964
-   Rival groups and their backers

There were two obstacles in the way of these objectives. First, ONUC could only take military action in self-defence. Second, it was not allowed to support one side at the expense of another. This led to difficulties when Lumumba asked ONUC to attack Katanga and force it to rejoin the Congo. When Dag Hammarskjöld refused to allow this, Lumumba suspected that the UN was siding with Katanga.

Disgusted by the UN's refusal to act, Lumumba turned for help to the Soviet Union. Using Soviet military equipment, Lumumba supporters attacked Katanga in August. When the attack failed, President Kasavubu dismissed Lumumba and allowed the chief of the Congolese army, Colonel Mobutu, to replace him in a military takeover. Lumumba set up a rival government in Stanleyville in Eastern province, but was murdered in January 1961 after being captured by mercenary soldiers in Katanga.

Civil war threatens

For the next six months, power was divided between four groups: Lumumba's supporters in Stanleyville; Mobutu's military government in Leopoldville; Tshombe's Katangan government in Elizabethville; and another breakaway government in Kasai province, led by a self-appointed king, Albert Kalonji.

To complicate matters further, the Stanleyville and Kasai groups were taking aid in the form of weapons and transport from the USSR. The Congo therefore seemed about to break into four separate countries, two backed by the USSR and Katanga by the Belgians. Fearing that civil war would follow such a break-up, the UN Security Council gave ONUC authority to use force to prevent civil war.

For the time being, ONUC did not have to use force for this purpose. In August 1961 three of the four groups came together to form a parliament in Leopoldville. Protected by UN troops, the parliament elected a new government led by Cyrille Adoula.

Katanga defeated

Adoula put all his efforts into defeating Tshombe's

Katanga province. Now that ONUC could attack as well as defend, he was able to get UN help for this. In August 1961 5,000 ONUC troops attacked Katanga in 'Operation Rumpunch'. But although they occupied several key points in the province, they failed to unseat Tshombe, who fled to nearby Rhodesia.

In an attempt to negotiate peace between Adoula and Tshombe, Dag Hammarskjöld flew to Rhodesia to talk to Tshombe, but was killed when his plane hit a tree on take-off and crashed in flames.

Under a new Secretary-General, U Thant of Burma, ONUC forces attacked Katanga again in December 1961. Although the fighting had no clear result, Tshombe agreed to negotiate with Adoula. Talks between them dragged on for a year until a third ONUC attack in late 1962 forced Tshombe to flee the country. Katanga was then re-united with the Congo in January 1963.

Achievements and failures

By this time, ONUC had achieved its main objectives. It had got rid of the Belgians. It had stopped the Soviet Union getting involved in the crisis. It had prevented a civil war and had re-united Katanga with the rest of the Congo. UN civil servants had also helped to run the country during the crisis and had prevented famine and epidemics by providing food and medical aid. ONUC was therefore disbanded, the last plane-load of troops leaving in mid-1964.

Not all members of the UN praised ONUC, however. Three nations, France, Belgium and the USSR, disagreed so strongly with its actions that they refused to contribute to the $400 million cost of the Congo operations. This brought the UN close to bankruptcy, and meant that ONUC had to be recalled early.

Even nations which supported ONUC had criticisms to make. Some blamed it for doing nothing to prevent the murder of Lumumba in 1961. Others criticised its attack on Katanga because it had shed blood in the name of peace. And many disliked the leading part which Dag Hammarskjöld had played in the crisis, feeling that he had exceeded his powers as Secretary-General.

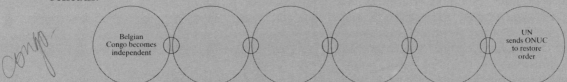

THE UN IN THE MIDDLE EAST SINCE 1967

The United Nations Emergency Force, UNEF (see page 11), stayed in Egypt from 1956 to 1967, supervising the ceasefire that followed the 1956 Suez War. However, tension between Israel and its Arab neighbours remained high, leading to war again in 1967.

The Six Day War of 1967

In May 1967 President Nasser of Egypt ordered UNEF to leave Egypt. It did so immediately, for the UN had agreed in 1956 to withdraw whenever asked to do so.

With UNEF no longer patrolling the Israel–Egypt border, tension rose. When Nasser then announced a blockade of the Straits of Tiran (see the map below), which Israeli ships used to get to and from the Red Sea, it seemed he was getting ready for war. The Israelis, fearing defeat if the Arabs had time to prepare for war, attacked Egypt, Jordan, Iraq and Syria before they could attack Israel.

The smaller but better-equipped and highly determined Israeli forces annihilated the armies of the Arab states. In only six days, Israel defeated them in battle and occupied the land shown on the map. Fighting ended when the UN Security Council ordered a ceasefire and drew up Resolution number 242, designed to restore peace to the Middle East.

Resolution 242

Resolution 242 called for:
1 the withdrawal of all Israeli forces from Arab land which they had occupied,
2 the right of every state in the area to exist in peace,
3 secure boundaries between each country,
4 free navigation in international waters,
5 a solution to the Palestinian refugee problem.
A Swedish statesman, Doctor Gunnar Jarring was given the task of trying to put the resolution into effect.

Israel and all the Arab states apart from Syria signed Resolution 242. As time went by, however, it became clear that Arabs and Israelis saw it in different ways. The Arabs were only interested in point 1 – the withdrawal of Israeli forces from Arab territory. The Israelis, on the other hand, said that there must be agreement on points 2–4 before they would hand back land to the Arabs. They also intended to keep any areas which they considered vital for their security.

These differing views of Resolution 242 made Jarring's task impossible. He commuted between the Arab states, New York and Jerusalem from 1968–72, holding talks between the two sides, but achieved little apart from an exchange of war prisoners.

The 1973 Arab–Israeli War

In 1973 Egypt's new President, Anwar Sadat, announced that the failure of all peace plans made it necessary for the Arabs to settle the problem with a new military offensive. The result was a third war, in October 1973, in which the Arab states invaded Israel.

As on previous occasions, the UN passed a peace resolution. Resolution 338 called for a ceasefire and for peace talks based on Resolution 242. A UN conference met in Geneva to try to turn this into a peace settlement, but with no success.

From then on, the search for peace was led by the United States. US Secretary of State Henry Kissinger flew back and forth between Israel and Egypt, helping the two sides arrange a withdrawal of their forces by talking separately to each in turn. As a result of this 'shuttle diplomacy' Israel and Egypt signed a Disengagement Agreement in January 1974. An agreement between Israel and Syria followed in May. As part of the agreements, a new 7,000-man UN Emergency Force, UNEF II, was stationed between Israel and Egypt, while a UN Disengagement Ob-

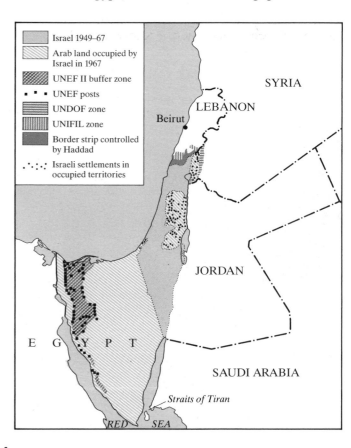

▒	Israel 1949–67
╱	Arab land occupied by Israel in 1967
▓	UNEF II buffer zone
• • •	UNEF posts
≡	UNDOF zone
⦀	UNIFIL zone
■	Border strip controlled by Haddad
∴	Israeli settlements in occupied territories

SYRIA

LEBANON

Beirut

JORDAN

E G Y P T

SAUDI ARABIA

Straits of Tiran

RED SEA

A UNDOF sentry outpost between Israel and Syria, 1972

server Force (UNDOF) of 1,250 men was sent to monitor the border between Israel and Syria.

The USA continued to lead the search for peace after this. In 1975 Dr Kissinger helped to arrange an agreement for Israel to withdraw from large parts of the Sinai desert. And in 1978, after President Sadat of Egypt announced that he would discuss peace in person with the Israelis, President Carter of the USA helped the two countries to make peace with each other in talks at Camp David in the USA.

Meanwhile, the UN General Assembly became increasingly hostile towards Israel. In 1975 it accused the Israeli government of racism and said that Palestinians had a right to return to their homes. In 1976 it said that the territories occupied by Israel should be handed over to the Palestine Liberation Organisation after an Israeli withdrawal. And in 1977 it criticised Israel's policy of creating settlements in the occupied territories (see the map opposite).

The UN and Lebanon

The Middle East conflict was most damaging in Lebanon. Since 1970, thousands of fighters belonging to the Palestine Liberation Organisation (PLO) had settled in Lebanon. From there they launched frequent guerilla raids on Israel. Israel replied with heavy air attacks on their bases.

This struggle became more intense when a civil war began in 1975 between Christian and Muslim Lebanese. Israel joined in this war by supporting pro-Israeli Christian forces in south Lebanon. In 1978 they invaded the country.

In an attempt to halt the invasion, the UN Security Council passed Resolution 425, calling upon Israel to withdraw, and sent a 6,000-strong UN Interim Force in Lebanon (UNIFIL) to be a buffer between Israeli and Lebanese forces. The Israelis agreed to leave the country, but only after they had given a 10-km strip of Lebanese territory on the border to the pro-Israeli Major Haddad, leader of a Christian militia. Haddad's men refused to allow UNIFIL into the strip, meaning that Israel could re-enter Lebanon whenever it liked.

The Israelis invaded Lebanon again in 1982. Their aim was to drive the PLO out of the capital, Beirut. After a brutal siege, the Israelis forced the PLO to evacuate the city. This was supervised by a 'Multi-National Force' of US, French and Italian troops organised by the UN. The MNF, joined by British troops, stayed on in Beirut from 1982–84 to try to keep the various Muslim and Christian groups, fighting in the civil war, apart. They were withdrawn in 1984 after this task proved impossible, and the civil war continued unabated in Beirut.

In southern Lebanon, UNIFIL remained on duty for the remainder of the 1980s. Some of the difficulties facing them can be seen in these news reports of 1986–87:

A 'The French contingent was singled out for a series of attacks in September; three French soldiers died when a bomb exploded as their jogging party passed along a road near Jouaiya. . . .'

B 'A hitherto unknown group, the 'Revolutionary Brigade for the Liberation of the Border Strip', warned on 3 September that it would treat the UNIFIL contingent as 'hostages' unless Israel agreed to implement UN Security Council Resolution 425 of 1978'.

C 'Three Fijian UNIFIL soldiers manning a UN checkpoint were killed on November 20 when a suicide car bomber blew up his vehicle. . . .'

D 'An Irish UNIFIL soldier was killed on January 10 1987 when Israeli tank fire hit a UN command post. An Israeli spokesman claimed that the Israeli commander had believed he was firing at a 'terrorist commando' position.'

Work section

A. 1. List at least four ways in which the UN has tried to restore peace in the Middle East since 1967.
   2. List ways in which the United States government has attempted to restore peace.
   3. Whose attempts to restore peace seem to have been most successful – the UN or the USA?

B. 1. What is 'UNIFIL' and what is its function?
   2. According to sources A to D, what problems does UNIFIL face in performing its function?
   3. What do sources A to D reveal about the composition of UNIFIL?

C. Study the photograph above, then answer these questions:
   1. What was UNDOF? How did its function differ from that of UNIFIL?
   2. What difficulties were these soldiers likely to face in performing this function?

UN PEACEKEEPING 1945–90: AN ASSESSMENT

During the lifetime of the UN, 1945 to the present, there have been more than 160 wars in the world. These conflicts have killed some 13.5 million people, driven millions from their homes, and caused incalculable damage to land and property. Since 1945 the world has experienced just twenty-six days without war.

What has the UN done to try to stop wars and to limit their effects? The map and the chart below show twenty-five of the conflicts in which the UN has tried to mediate. You should study them, in conjunction with the questions which follow, in order to judge the success of the UN as a world peacekeeper.

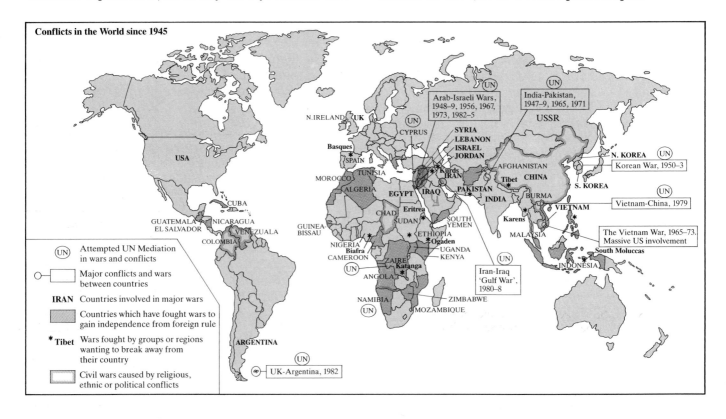

Attempted UN mediation in conflicts since 1945

	Time	Place	Nature of conflict	UN action	Results
A	1946	Iran	see page 6	– – –	– – –
B	1946–8	Greece	see page 6	– – –	– – –
C	1947	Kashmir	A dispute between India and Pakistan over the ownership of the state of Kashmir.	Security Council created a Commission on India and Pakistan (UNCIP) which arranged a ceasefire (Jan 1949) and set up a UN Military Observer Group (UNMOGIP) to monitor it.	Ceasefire held for sixteen years, but UNCIP could not persuade either side to withdraw forces from Kashmir during that time.
D	1947–9	Indonesia	see page 6	– – –	– – –
E	1947–9	Palestine	see pages 6–7	– – –	– – –
F	1950–3	Korea	see pages 8–9	– – –	– – –

G	1956	Hungary	Soviet troops invaded Hungary to crush a revolt against Soviet control of the country.	Resolution by Security Council called for withdrawal of Soviet troops. General Assembly set up a Committee of Investigation.	Soviet delegate in Security Council vetoed the resolution and refused to co-operate with the Committee of Investigation.
H	1956	Suez/Sinai	see page 11	———	———
I	1958	Lebanon	An anti-government rebellion broke out in 1958. The Lebanese government claimed that neighbouring Syria was giving weapons and money to the rebels, and asked for UN help against this interference.	The Security Council created a 100-man UNOGIL (UN Observation Group in Lebanon) to ensure that no Syrian arms or supplies were taken across the border.	UNOGIL monitored the Syria–Lebanon border from June–November 1958 and reported little Syrian cross-border activity. Lebanon accepted the report and UNOGIL left in Dec. 1958.
J	1960–4	Congo	see pages 12–13	———	———
K	1962	West Irian (Indonesia)	A dispute between Indonesia and the Dutch Netherlands over the ownership of West Irian (Dutch New Guinea; see map on page 6).	After mediation by Secretary-General, Netherlands agreed to transfer West Irian to Indonesia. General Assembly then set up UNTEA (UN Temporary Authority) to govern the area until the transfer.	UNTEA administered West Irian for the next seven months, then transferred power smoothly to Indonesia.
L	1962	Yemen	A civil war began in Yemen in 1962, with Egypt backing Republicans on one side and Saudi Arabia backing Royalists on the other. The Royalists appealed for UN help against Egypt.	Egypt and Saudi Arabia agreed without UN involvement to leave Yemen. The Security Council then set up UNYOM (UN Yemen Observation Mission) to observe their withdrawal.	UNYOM stayed in Yemen until September 1964 when it reported a substantial reduction in Egypt's forces. It was then withdrawn.
M	1963	Cyprus	Following independence from Britain in 1960, civil war began between the Greek and Turkish communities in Cyprus in 1963.	The Security Council sent a 6,000-man buffer force to Cyprus (UNFICYP) to keep the two communities apart.	UNFICYP kept the two sides apart for the next ten years, but could not stop violence flaring up again in 1974 (see T below).
N	1965–6	Dominican Republic	Civil war flared up after the overthrow of the President in 1965. US forces intervened to prevent a suspected Communist takeover.	Secretary-General sent a representative to the Dominican Republic (DOMREP) to observe the situation.	DOMREP stayed until 1966 and was then withdrawn. (All peace-keeping was done by an 'Inter-American Peace Force' sent by the Organisation of American States).
O	1966–80	Zimbabwe (Rhodesia)	A white minority in British–run Rhodesia proclaimed independence and set up a white minority government to prevent the black majority gaining voting rights.	Security Council condemned their action and imposed economic sanctions on Rhodesia to cut off essential supplies such as oil.	Sanctions were ineffective because white South Africa refused to apply them. White rule continued until defeated by 'Patriotic Front' forces in a seven-year guerilla war, 1973–80.
P	1967–	Kashmir	A revival of the dispute between India and Pakistan which began in 1947 (see C above).	UN ordered them back to the 1947 ceasefire line and set up a UN India and Pakistan Observation Mission (UNPOM) to supervise the ceasefire.	India and Pakistan agreed to a truce after talks in the USSR. UNPOM and UNMOGIP supervised the withdrawal of both sides.
Q	1967	Middle East	see page 14	———	———
R	1971–	Kashmir	A revival of the dispute which began in 1947 (see C and P above).	UN ordered a ceasefire.	India and Pakistan agreed to withdraw to the 1947 ceasefire line. UNMOGIP observed the withdrawal and has stayed there ever since.
S	1973	Middle East	see page 14	———	———
T	1974–	Cyprus	Greek Cypriots tried to unite Cyprus with Greece. In response, Turkish Cypriots helped by the Turkish army seized northern Cyprus.	UN arranged a ceasefire. UNFICYP (see M above) took up stations along the line dividing north from south.	The ceasefire has held ever since. 2,500 UNFICYP troops remain there today.

U	1975	East Timor (Indonesia)	Indonesian troops occupied East Timor, a Portuguese colony, and declared it part of Indonesia.	Resolutions by General Assembly and Security Council called for the withdrawal of Indonesian troops.	Indonesia ignored the resolutions and kept its troops in East Timor.
V	1979–88	Afghanistan	Soviet troops invaded and occupied Afghanistan to prop up a pro-Soviet government.	Resolutions by Security Council and General Assembly called for Soviet troops to withdraw.	The Soviets vetoed the Security Council resolution and kept troops in Afghanistan until 1988.
W	1980–88	Iraq-Iran	Iraq invaded Iran and occupied the Shatt-al-Arab waterway as part of a long running territorial dispute.	Security Council passed a resolution calling for a ceasefire between the two countries.	Both ignored the resolution and full-scale war lasted for the next 8 years. The UN supervised a ceasefire after Iran capitulated in 1988.
X	1982–5	Lebanon	see page 15	–––	–––
Y	1982	Falkland Islands	A conflict between the UK and Argentina over ownership of the Falkland Islands after Argentine forces invaded and occupied them.	A Security Council resolution demanded the withdrawal of Argentine forces and called upon both sides to settle the dispute peacefully.	Argentine forces ignored the resolution and stayed on the islands. Britain retook the islands by force.
Z	1989	Namibia	see page 25	–––	–––

Assessment exercise

A.
1. List the five different types of armed conflict shown on the map on page 16.
2. What, according to the map, has been the most common type of conflict since 1945?
3. In which types of conflict has the UN tried to make peace?
4. Suggest why the UN has not often tried to make peace in the other types of conflict.
5. Which parts of the world have seen most conflicts since 1945? Which have been least affected?

B.
1. Make a grid like the one below, showing the different ways in which the UN has tried to keep peace, and the conflicts, A to Y, in which it has been involved.
2. Taking information from the chart on pages 16–18 and, where necessary, from Chapters 3–7 of this book, mark the grid to show the action or actions which the UN took in each conflict.
3. Where UN action was effective, show this on your grid by marking the box in a different colour.

Action ▽ Conflict ▷	A	B	C	D	E	F	G	H	I	J	K	L	M	N	O	P	Q	R	S	T	U	V	W	X	Y	Z
Resolution calling for a ceasefire or troop withdrawal																										
Arranged a ceasefire or truce																										
Set up a committee (e.g. investigation, conciliation)																										
Sent observers to monitor a ceasefire or other situation																										
Sent an armed force to be a 'buffer' between two sides																										
Created a UN army to restore order by force																										
Imposed economic sanctions on a country																										
Did nothing																										

4. Judging by your completed grid,
   (a) what kind of action has the UN used most frequently to deal with conflicts?
   (b) what kind of action has proved most effective?
   (c) what kind of action has proved least effective?
5. Read the following opinion written by an American historian in 1982:
   'If one adopts an ideal standard – for example, the expectations of the drafters of the UN Charter – there is no question that the United Nations has failed abysmally to cope satisfactorily with . . . international violence.'
   Using your completed grid, give evidence to (a) support the above opinion, (b) disagree with it.
6. In the light of your answer to the above questions assess how effective you think the UN has been as a peace-keeping body since 1945.

PART TWO

THE 'NON-POLITICAL' UN

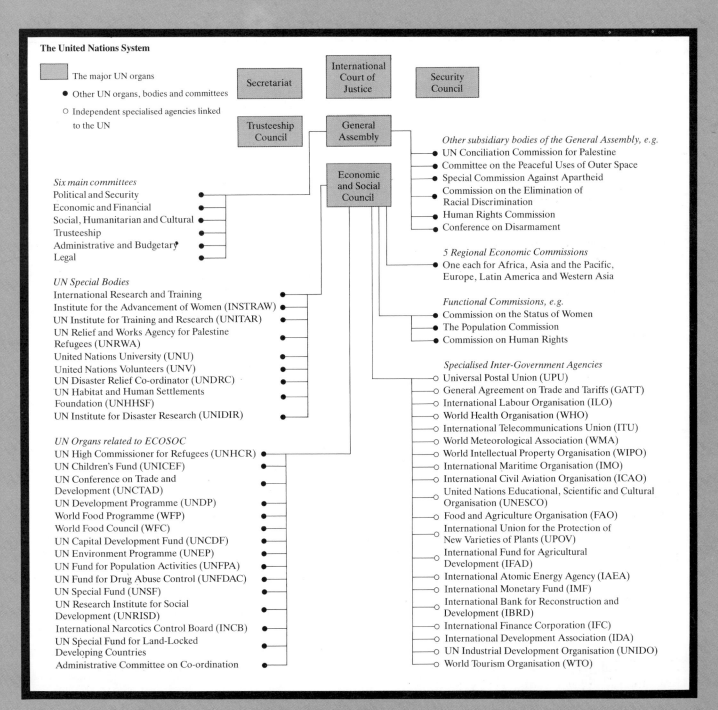

The United Nations System

- ▨ The major UN organs
- ● Other UN organs, bodies and committees
- ○ Independent specialised agencies linked to the UN

Secretariat

International Court of Justice

Security Council

Trusteeship Council

General Assembly

Economic and Social Council

Other subsidiary bodies of the General Assembly, e.g.
- UN Conciliation Commission for Palestine
- Committee on the Peaceful Uses of Outer Space
- Special Commission Against Apartheid
- Commission on the Elimination of Racial Discrimination
- Human Rights Commission
- Conference on Disarmament

Six main committees
- Political and Security
- Economic and Financial
- Social, Humanitarian and Cultural
- Trusteeship
- Administrative and Budgetary
- Legal

5 Regional Economic Commissions
- One each for Africa, Asia and the Pacific, Europe, Latin America and Western Asia

Functional Commissions, e.g.
- Commission on the Status of Women
- The Population Commission
- Commission on Human Rights

UN Special Bodies
- International Research and Training Institute for the Advancement of Women (INSTRAW)
- UN Institute for Training and Research (UNITAR)
- UN Relief and Works Agency for Palestine Refugees (UNRWA)
- United Nations University (UNU)
- United Nations Volunteers (UNV)
- UN Disaster Relief Co-ordinator (UNDRC)
- UN Habitat and Human Settlements Foundation (UNHHSF)
- UN Institute for Disaster Research (UNIDIR)

Specialised Inter-Government Agencies
- Universal Postal Union (UPU)
- General Agreement on Trade and Tariffs (GATT)
- International Labour Organisation (ILO)
- World Health Organisation (WHO)
- International Telecommunications Union (ITU)
- World Meteorological Association (WMA)
- World Intellectual Property Organisation (WIPO)
- International Maritime Organisation (IMO)
- International Civil Aviation Organisation (ICAO)
- United Nations Educational, Scientific and Cultural Organisation (UNESCO)
- Food and Agriculture Organisation (FAO)
- International Union for the Protection of New Varieties of Plants (UPOV)
- International Fund for Agricultural Development (IFAD)
- International Atomic Energy Agency (IAEA)
- International Monetary Fund (IMF)
- International Bank for Reconstruction and Development (IBRD)
- International Finance Corporation (IFC)
- International Development Association (IDA)
- UN Industrial Development Organisation (UNIDO)
- World Tourism Organisation (WTO)

UN Organs related to ECOSOC
- UN High Commissioner for Refugees (UNHCR)
- UN Children's Fund (UNICEF)
- UN Conference on Trade and Development (UNCTAD)
- UN Development Programme (UNDP)
- World Food Programme (WFP)
- World Food Council (WFC)
- UN Capital Development Fund (UNCDF)
- UN Environment Programme (UNEP)
- UN Fund for Population Activities (UNFPA)
- UN Fund for Drug Abuse Control (UNFDAC)
- UN Special Fund (UNSF)
- UN Research Institute for Social Development (UNRISD)
- International Narcotics Control Board (INCB)
- UN Special Fund for Land-Locked Developing Countries
- Administrative Committee on Co-ordination

So far in this book you have read about the political work of the UN – that is, its attempts to keep peace between nations. Also very important is its non-political work, which is meant to improve the living standards, work conditions, health, rights and education of people everywhere.

You can see from the diagram above that the UN's non-political work is done by a network of special bodies, organs and specialised agencies. Between them they provide a very wide range of services – social, economic and financial. Part Two of this book will show how some of these bodies have been very successful, and are respected in every part of the world. Several, however, have lost the respect of some countries, and find their work being obstructed and opposed by them. It will be for you to judge whether the successes of these 'non-political' bodies have been greater or less than their failures.

9

UN MEMBERSHIP: GROWTH AND CHANGE

When the UN was founded in 1945 it had fifty-one member states. The powerful western states – Britain, France, the USA and the USSR – and their allies were in the majority. This allowed them to dominate the activities of the UN in its early years.

Now there are 159 states in the UN. All but nine countries in the world are members. This increase has been due mainly to the process of decolonisation.

Decolonisation and the UN

Before 1945, over half the world belonged to European empires. Most of Africa and much of Asia was divided into colonies and dominions run by the British and French, the Belgians, Dutch and Germans, the Spanish and the Portuguese.

In the forty years after 1945, the Europeans gave most of their colonies independence. As each colony became independent, it was able to join the UN as a sovereign state, equal to all the others in status and voting rights. The graph below shows when and where this rapid growth in membership took place.

As a result, the powerful western states and their allies ceased to be a majority in the UN. In their place, the new African and Asian countries formed powerful blocs, or groupings, which allowed them to dominate the UN's activities.

Power blocs in the UN

There are eight main blocs in the UN. They are similar in many ways to political parties in a national parliament. The largest of these groupings is the Developing Nations bloc, consisting of 125 African, Asian, Caribbean and Latin American states which share a number of basic aims. Their aims can be seen in this extract from the Algiers Charter which they drew up in 1967:

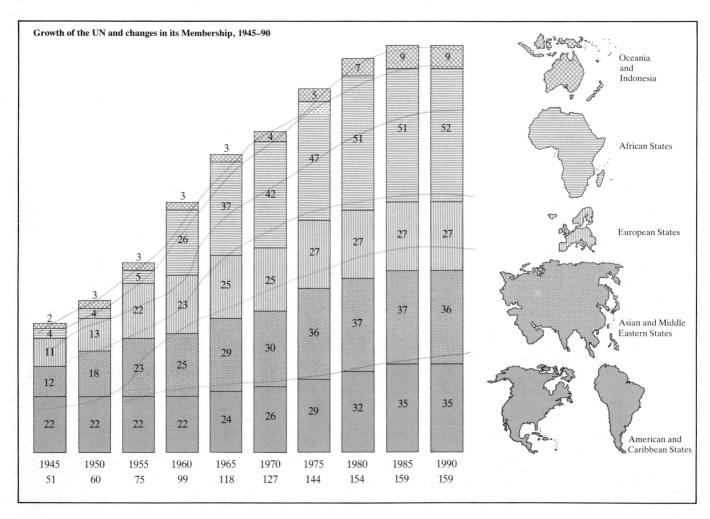

Growth of the UN and changes in its Membership, 1945–90

1945	1950	1955	1960	1965	1970	1975	1980	1985	1990
51	60	75	99	118	127	144	154	159	159

Oceania and Indonesia

African States

European States

Asian and Middle Eastern States

American and Caribbean States

'The representatives of developing countries, . . . determined to pursue their joint efforts towards economic and social development, peace and prosperity . . . deem it their duty to call the attention of the international community to the following facts:

The lot of more than a billion people in the developing world continues to deteriorate . . .

The rate of economic growth of the developing world has slowed down and the disparity between it and the affluent (*wealthy*) world is widening;

While the developed countries are adding annually approximately 60 dollars to the per capita [*per person*] income of their people, the average increase of per capita income in the developing world amounts to less than 2 dollars per annum . . .

The purchasing power of exports from developing countries has been steadily declining. . .

Although modern technology offers developing countries great possibilities to accelerate their economic development, its benefits are largely by-passing them. . .

The virtual stagnation in the production of foodstuffs in developing countries, in contrast with the rapid increase in population, has aggravated the chronic conditions of under-nourishment and malnutritition.'

The second largest bloc in the UN consists of ninety-nine states which belong to the Non-Aligned Movement. This is a group of mostly African and Asian countries which avoid commiting themselves to any military alliance.

Bringing together countries in North Africa, the Middle East and Asia is the Islamic Conference of forty-one Islamic states.

Finally, there are blocs representing each major region of the world such as:

- The African group (50 states)
- The Latin American group (33 states)
- The Western European states (22 states)
- The Arab group (21 states)

Voting in the UN

In the UN General Assembly, each member nation has one vote. This one-nation, one-vote principle is also used in many of the UN organs and specialised agencies. It is not used, as you have found out, in the Security Council where five permanent members can veto any resolution.

Many developing countries want to change the voting system so that all UN organs and agencies make decisions on the one-nation, one-vote basis. This would give them a greater say in UN affairs and would reduce the power of the developed countries.

Most of the developed nations disagree. The USA, for example, says it should have a greater say than the developing countries because it is of greater importance in the world, has a large population and gives more money to UN funds than any other country. This can be seen clearly in source B:

B 20 members' contributions (%) to the UN budget in 1985:

Angola	0.01	Libya	0.26
Bolivia	0.01	Mexico	0.88
Chile	0.07	Netherlands	1.78
Denmark	0.75	Pakistan	0.06
Ethiopia	0.01	Saudi Arabia	0.86
France	6.51	Sweden	1.32
India	0.36	Tanzania	0.01
Italy	3.74	USSR	10.52
Japan	10.32	United Kingdom	4.67
Kenya	0.01	USA	25.00

The US Congress therefore declared in 1985 that:

C 'Voting rights (in the UN should be) proportionate to the contribution of each member state to the budget of the United Nations and its specialised agencies.'

As we shall see, the argument about voting in the UN has seriously affected its non-political work.

Work section

A Study the table opposite, then answer these questions:
1. Which region of the world dominated the UN's membership in 1945?
2. Give an example, taken from Part One of this book, of how that region's dominance affected the peace-keeping work of the UN in 1945–60.
3. Which area of the world dominated the UN's membership in 1990?
4. In which years did it become dominant? How do you explain its rise to dominance at that time?

B. Study source A, then answer these questions:
1. Under the following headings, state briefly what the 'developing nations' had in common according to source A: economic growth, people's incomes, exports, technology, food supplies, health.
2. Using source A for information, list the differences between 'developed' and 'developing' nations.

C 1. In source B, identify ten 'developing' countries and ten 'developed' countries.
2. How might an American use the figures in source B as evidence that the USA should have more voting rights than other countries in the UN?
3. How might an 'undeveloped' country's government argue against this?

10

THE SPECIALISED AGENCIES

Much of the UN's non-political work is done by eighteen Specialised Agencies. As the panel opposite shows, they deal with a great variety of social, economic and technical problems. Each Agency is an independent, self-governing body which has an agreement to work with the UN. The Economic and Social Council helps them work together by acting as an intermediary between them.

Aims of the Agencies

Many of the Specialised Agencies were set up shortly after the Second World War. What were their founders hoping to achieve? We can see some of their aims in the opening words of each agency's constitution, or set of rules. Sources A to D are four examples:

A **International Labour Organisation (1944)**
'All human beings, irrespective of race, creed or sex, have the right to pursue both their material well-being and their spiritual development in conditions of freedom and dignity, of economic security and equal opportunity.'

B **UNESCO (1944)**
'Since wars begin in the minds of men, it is in the minds of men that the defences of peace must be constructed . . .

The purpose of this organisation is to contribute to peace and security by promoting collaboration among the nations through education, science and culture in order to further universal respect for justice, for the law and for human rights.'

C **World Health Organisation (1946)**
'Health is a state of complete physical, mental and social well-being, and not merely the absence of disease. The enjoyment of the highest attainable standard of health is one of the fundamental rights of every human being.'

D **International Atomic Energy Authority (1957)**
'The IAEA shall seek to accelerate and enlarge the contribution of atomic energy to peace, health and properity throughout the world.'

Achievements

Some of the Agencies have been very successful in their work.

In 1967 the WHO started a global campaign to wipe out the disease smallpox in the next ten years.

In that year, 131,418 cases were reported in forty-three countries. By 1984, not a single case of smallpox occurred anywhere in the world. WHO was therefore able to report that the smallpox virus was extinct.

The ILO, by 1980, had drawn up 153 Conventions (*sets of rules*) on a wide range of labour issues. These included maximum hours of work, working conditions, trade union rights, old age and unemployment insurance. As the 151 countries which belong to ILO are bound by its rules to put these conventions into effect, they have led to improvements in working peoples' lives almost everywhere in the world.

All the agencies have their success stories, some modest and some of world importance. Several of the Agencies, however, have run into major difficulties. This is particularly true of UNESCO.

Specialised Agencies of the United Nations

The 'Big Five'
ILO – International Labour Organisation.
Works to improve workers' conditions, rights, living standards, wages and insurance throughout the world.
WHO – World Health Organisation.
Co-ordinates medical research, monitors infectious diseases, helps developing countries organise health services, mounts health campaigns.
UNESCO – United Nations Educational, Scientific and Cultural Organisation.
Promotes co-operation among nations through education, science and culture.
FAO – Food and Agriculture Organisation.
Works to raise levels of nutrition, to improve production and distribution of food, and to improve conditions of rural people.
UNIDO – UN Industrial Development Organisation.
Promotes industry in developing countries.

The technical organisations
IAEA – International Atomic Energy Agency.
Promotes the peaceful uses of atomic energy.
UPU – Universal Postal Union.
Works for the improvement of world postal services.
ITU – International Telecommunication Union.
Organises and improves the world's telephone and telegraph network, and monitors international radio frequencies.
WMO – World Meteorological Organisation.
Monitors weather from a world-wide network of stations and encourages nations to work together in forecasting.
WIPO – World Intellectual Property Organisation.
Protects inventions, patents, copyrights, trademarks, artistic and literary works against illegal copying.

IMO – International Maritime Organisation.
Encourages safe shipping and navigation practices.
ICAO – International Civil Aviation Organisation.
Works for safety in air navigation transport.

The economic organisations
IFAD – International Fund for Agricultural Development.
Lends money to developing nations to improve farming.
IMF – International Monetary Fund.
Lends money to nations having balance of payments problems, works to stabilise currency exchange rates, and promotes monetary co-operation between nations.
IBRD – International Bank for Reconstruction.
Lends money to member nations for major construction and development projects – e.g. roads, dams, railways.
IFC – International Finance Corporation.
Invests money in private enterprises or joint government/private enterprises in developing countries.
IDA – International Development Association.
Promotes economic development in developing countries by lending them money on easy repayment terms.
GATT – General Agreement on Tariffs and Trade.
International treaty laying down rules of world trade.

UNESCO

Formed in 1945 at the end of the Second World War, UNESCO was composed mainly of western European countries, plus the USA and Canada.

In its early years, UNESCO organised many projects aimed at healing the hatreds that divided many European peoples after the War. It also fostered many projects in the European colonies, soon to become independent, such as literacy programmes to help people to learn to read and write.

During the 1960s and 1970s, UNESCO's membership grew. This was partly because the USSR and eastern European countries joined, but chiefly it was due to the admission of newly-independent African and Asian states. By the 1980s the original western European and American members were a minority.

This led to dissent in UNESCO. Many of the new members, especially those from Asia and Africa, were hostile to western European ideas about what

NEW VARIETIES OF RICE MAY INCREASE THE FOOD SUPPLIES IN SOUTH EAST ASIA

Rice is the staple food of seventy per cent of Asia's people. But while the population has increased, the rice output is still below pre-war level. Millions live on the edge of famine. Indian agricultural experts, with assistance from the Food and Agriculture Organization of the United Nations (FAO), are working to develop a hybrid of Japanese and Indian rice which might greatly increase the yield.

A UN poster publicising the activities of the Food and Agriculture Organisation, 1966

UNESCO should do. In 1977, for example, they attempted to set up a 'New World Information and Communications Order'. This would take control of communications satellites, television and radio services, press networks, etc, away from the developed western nations and give it to the developing countries.

The original western members disagreed with such schemes. They also resented the fact that they paid much more into UNESCO's funds than the others. The USA, for example, in 1984 paid 25 per cent of the total budget. As a result, the USA and Britain withdrew from membership of UNESCO in 1985.

Other Specialised Agencies faced similar problems. The USA withdrew from ILO in 1977, complaining that it did little about breaches of human rights in the USSR and eastern Europe. WHO ran into opposition from the western powers when it made a study of 'the effects of nuclear war on health and health services': they claimed this was a political issue that had nothing to do with WHO. In all such cases, the complaint of the western powers was that the developing nations were 'politicising' the Agencies. By this they meant that the Agencies were being involved in political matters that were none of their business.

Work section

A. Refer to the table opposite. Which of the Specialised Agencies do you think could help to deal with the following problems? (In some cases, more than one Agency might help.)
   The spread of the AIDS virus   The exploitation of child workers
   Famine caused by drought in Africa   Flooding in Bangladesh

B. 1. Describe in your own words the aims of the scheme shown in the poster above.
   2. Suggest what the FAO can do to help achieve these aims that a national government cannot do by itself.

C Study sources A to D.
   1. What general aims do these Specialised Agencies share in common?
   2. What difficulties is a Specialised Agency likely to meet in putting such aims into effect?

11

THE UN AND DECOLONISATION

One of the UN's closest concerns after 1945 was **decolonisation**. This was the process by which people living in foreign-run colonies gained independence and the right to govern their own affairs.

The colonies in 1945

In 1945 the world contained more than eighty colonies belonging to seven European countries. They included a third of the world's population, covered a third of the world's land surface, and provided huge quantities of raw materials. The colonies thus made Europe rich and powerful.

By the end of World War Two in 1945, it was becoming difficult for the Europeans to keep their colonies. The War had badly disrupted their control of them, and many colonial people were demanding independence.

The UN Trusteeship system

The UN approached the problem of the colonies by setting up an **International Trusteeship System**.

The basic idea of the Trusteeship System was stated in the UN's Charter. It said that UN members which owned colonies had 'a sacred trust' to look after the well-being of the people who lived there and to prepare them for independence.

The UN Charter defined three categories of trust territory. In the first were the mandated territories of the League of Nations, forerunner of the UN. These were colonies taken from Germany and Turkey at the end of the First World War and put under the control of the main victors – Britain, France, the USA and Japan. They were to help the people of the colonies run their affairs until they could do so themselves. A colony run like this was called a mandate.

In the second category were territories taken from the states defeated in the Second World War – Germany, Italy and Japan. And in the third category were any other territories that the European powers volunteered to place under the UN Trusteeship system.

By 1950 the UN had approved a total of eleven trusteeships. All but one were former mandates. To govern these territories, the UN appointed member nations to be trustees. A **Trusteeship Council**, meeting at least once a year, was given the job of checking that the trustees were doing their job properly.

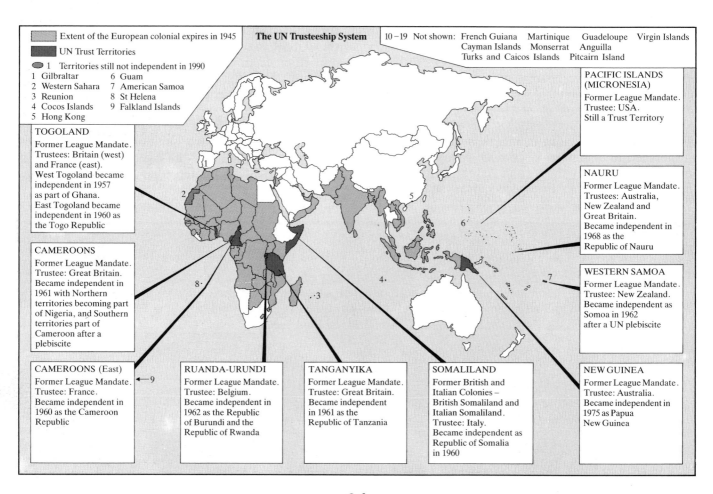

The UN Trusteeship System

Extent of the European colonial expires in 1945

UN Trust Territories

1 Territories still not independent in 1990

1 Gilbraltar
2 Western Sahara
3 Reunion
4 Cocos Islands
5 Hong Kong
6 Guam
7 American Samoa
8 St Helena
9 Falkland Islands

10 – 19 Not shown: French Guiana Martinique Guadeloupe Virgin Islands Cayman Islands Monserrat Anguilla Turks and Caicos Islands Pitcairn Island

TOGOLAND
Former League Mandate. Trustees: Britain (west) and France (east). West Togoland became independent in 1957 as part of Ghana. East Togoland became independent in 1960 as the Togo Republic

CAMEROONS
Former League Mandate. Trustee: Great Britain. Became independent in 1961 with Northern territories becoming part of Nigeria, and Southern territories part of Cameroon after a plebiscite

CAMEROONS (East)
Former League Mandate. Trustee: France. Became independent in 1960 as the Cameroon Republic

RUANDA-URUNDI
Former League Mandate. Trustee: Belgium. Became independent in 1962 as the Republic of Burundi and the Republic of Rwanda

TANGANYIKA
Former League Mandate. Trustee: Great Britain. Became independent in 1961 as the Republic of Tanzania

SOMALILAND
Former British and Italian Colonies – British Somaliland and Italian Somaliland. Trustee: Italy. Became independent as Republic of Somalia in 1960

PACIFIC ISLANDS (MICRONESIA)
Former League Mandate. Trustee: USA. Still a Trust Territory

NAURU
Former League Mandate. Trustees: Australia, New Zealand and Great Britain. Became independent in 1968 as the Republic of Nauru

WESTERN SAMOA
Former League Mandate. Trustee: New Zealand. Became independent as Samoa in 1962 after a UN plebiscite

NEW GUINEA
Former League Mandate. Trustee: Australia. Became independent in 1975 as Papua New Guinea

TO YOU WHO LIVE IN THE NORTHERN CAMEROONS TRUST TERRITORY AND WHO REGISTERED AS VOTERS THIS YEAR

Come early on Saturday the 7th November and decide whether you want your country to become part of the Northern Region next year OR whether you want to leave consideration of this matter to some other time in the future.

This is what we want you to do:

Come here with your registration cards early on Saturday the 7th of November.

The Polling Officer will check your name against the list of those registered to vote.

He will give you a ballot paper & tell you to go into the polling booth ALONE.

If you want your country to join Northern Nigeria next year put the ballot paper in the WHITE box. If you want to postpone consideration put it into the ORANGE COLOURED box.

You *cannot* vote twice.
You *cannot* vote on behalf of anyone who is ill.
You *cannot* vote on behalf of anyone who has died.
You *cannot* vote on behalf of anyone else.
You *cannot* enter the polling station after 5 p.m.

You can only vote where you were registered.

THIS HAS NOTHING TO DO WITH THE FEDERAL ELECTION

Poster advertising a UN supervised plebiscite in the British-run Trust Territory of Northern Cameroons, 1961

The other colonies

As you can see from the map, none of the European powers placed any of their own colonies under the Trusteeship System. Instead, they gave their colonies independence as and when they chose to do so.

While the UN was dominated by the western nations (see page 20) there was little it could do to change this. But from 1960 onwards, many colonies became independent and joined the UN. Under their influence the UN began to criticise members which still kept their colonies. In 1960, for example, a **UN Declaration on Independence** stated that colonialism was a denial of human rights and a bar to world peace. In 1961 the UN set up a Committee on Decolonisation to monitor the progress of colonies towards independence.

By 1990 the process of decolonisation was nearly over. As the map shows, only a handful of colonies remained as loose ends of the European empires.

The loose ends of the empires

In a few cases, these loose ends of the empires continued to cause major problems. The longest lasting of these concerned **Namibia** in Southern Africa.

Namibia was a League of Nations Mandate, governed by South Africa, from 1919–45, becoming a UN Trust Territory in 1946. When South Africa tried to make Namibia into one of its own provinces in 1946, the UN terminated its Trusteeship.

South Africa ignored the UN's action and kept its forces in Namibia. In 1964 it extended its policy of apartheid into Namibia by dividing the country into non-white 'homelands' and exclusive white-only areas.

The UN tried many ways of persuading the South Africans to leave Namibia. It set up a Special Commission on Namibia in 1966. It recognised the South West African People's Organisation (SWAPO) as the true voice of the Namibian people, and gave it support when it began an armed struggle against South African troops.

The South Africans ignored the UN and remained in illegal possession of Namibia, saying that Cuban troops in Angola would help Angolan Communists to over-run Namibia if they left the country. The UN made a breakthrough in 1988 when it persuaded Angola, Cuba and South Africa to accept UN-supervised elections prior to independence for Namibia. However, when UN forces arrived in Namibia in 1989 to supervise its transition to independence, South African troops engaged SWAPO guerillas in heavy fighting. The UN forces were unable to stop these clashes in which over 2,000 SWAPO fighters died before Namibia finally became independent in 1990.

Work section

A   Study the poster above, then answer these questions:
1. Explain in your own words the meaning of the term 'Trust Territory' in the headline.
2. How does the poster suggest that the people of Northern Cameroons had little political experience?
3. What evidence is there in the poster that the British Trustees were helping the people of Northern Cameroons to prepare for independence and self-government?

B.   Study the map opposite, then answer these questions:
1. How many Trusteeships did the UN create?
2. What did these Trusteeships have in common?
3. Roughly how many colonies remained outside the Trusteeship system?
4. Suggest why the European colonial powers were willing to be Trustees of UN Trust Territories, but were not willing to put their own colonies into Trusteeship.
5. In your opinion, how successful has the UN Trusteeship system been? Explain your view.

12

THE UN IN CRISIS

As the UN grew during the 1960s and 1970s, so did the problems facing it. By the 1980s it looked likely to collapse under the weight of those problems.

The 'New International Economic Order'

The most difficult problem concerned the state of the world's economy. Many developing nations in the southern regions of the world were growing steadily poorer while the developed nations of the northern regions were growing richer.

This widening gap between North and South could be seen in many aspects of the world economy. The South in the 1980s was producing only a fifth of the world's annual output of $8.8 trillion. Average life expectancy in the South was sixteen years lower than in the North, while infant mortality was five times higher. Some 800 million people in the South were living in absolute poverty, and over 460 million were malnourished. To make matters worse, many Southern countries which had borrowed money from the North to develop their economies were being crushed by their debt repayments.

The developing nations in the UN tried to tackle these problems through UNCTAD, the UN Conference on Trade and Development. But, all too often, members failed to reach any decision at the annual conference. Critics said that UNCTAD meant 'Under No Circumstances Take Any Decision'.

In 1974, however, UNCTAD produced a highly detailed Declaration calling for a **New International Economic Order**. This called for the complete re-organisation of the world's trade, transport, industry, agriculture, money and technology to help the developing nations.

To look into how this might be done, the IMF (International Monetary Fund) set up a Commission on International Development Issues. In 1980, it produced a report entitled *North–South: A Programme for Survival*, calling for a big transfer of resources to the developing countries, a world energy programme, a global food programme, and a reform of the economic system.

Little came of the demand for a New International Economic Order. The wealthy Northern states looked on it with great suspicion. They feared, for example, that the NIEO would allow Northern-owned businesses in developing countries to be nationalised. Also damaging to the NIEO was a slump in the world economy in the early 1980s. This led many countries to take self-protection measures at the expense of poorer countries – for example, putting controls on their imports.

Even when the developed nations in the North recovered from the slump, little was done to put NIEO into effect. Helped by the World bank and IMF, they put more effort into making sure that developing countries with big debts paid them back.

The politicisation of the UN

A second problem troubling the UN in the 1980s was the continuing accusation that it was becoming 'politicised'. By this, its critics meant that some UN agencies and organs were involved in political issues that were none of their business (see page 23).

The first issue that led to this accusation was the Arab–Israeli conflict. Following Israel's occupation of land belonging to Syria, Jordan and Egypt in 1967 (see page 14), the UN became increasingly hostile to Israel. The General Assembly, for example, passed a resolution in 1975 saying that Israel's policy towards the neighbouring Arabs was 'racist'. Following this, several UN agencies and organs adopted anti-Israeli policies. The ILO, for example, claimed that Israel was violating trade union rights in the occupied territories, while the WHO expressed concern at the poor health of Arabs living under Israeli occupation.

A second issue leading to the charge of 'politicisation' was South Africa's policy of apartheid, which separates the people of South Africa according to skin colour. In an attempt to bring an end to apartheid, the UN repeatedly condemned the South African government, while six of the Specialised

An African cartoon published in the magazine Jeune Afrique *in 1970.*

Apartheid in action on a South African railway station. A photograph published in 1985 by the International Labour Organisation in its information pack Human Rights and the ILO

Agencies excluded South Africa from their work. Critics of the UN claimed that they did so for political reasons that had nothing to do with their work.

Many charges of 'politicisation' are made against the developing countries bloc by the USA and other western powers. The developing countries, however, have their own charges to make against the USA. They have claimed, for example, that the USA uses its influence to stop the World Bank Agencies (IMF, IBRD, IDF) lending money to countries it does not like. Among the countries that have faced US opposition in the World Bank are Vietnam, Cuba and Nicaragua, which have Communist governments. The developing countries complain that the USA has blocked loans to such countries as a way of hindering the growth of Communism.

Arguments about 'politicisation' came to a head in the 1980s, and helped bring about a great financial crisis in the UN.

The UN's financial crisis

Since the 1960s the UN had run up debts of $750 million, caused largely by the refusal of some members to pay for activities of which they disapproved. (The USSR, France and Belgium, for example, refused to pay any of the costs of the UN's intervention in the Congo in 1960–64.)

The situation reached crisis point in 1986 when the USA withheld $100 million from UN funds – half its yearly contribution. It did so largely because it resented the activities of the developing nations in the UN. In common with the other twenty members who paid 85 per cent of the UN's yearly budget, the USA objected to such policies as the New International Economic Order and to the politicisation of the UN Agencies.

As a result of its financial crisis, the UN had to slash its spending. Several major projects were cancelled, many other activities were trimmed, and 1,700 UN staff were dismissed.

The UN thus entered the fifth decade of its life with a very uncertain future. Divided on nearly every issue between North and South and rich and poor, it found it increasingly difficult to take action on the growing number of problems brought before it.

Work section

A. Study the cartoon opposite, then answer these questions:
1. What point is made by the cartoon?
2. What has the UN done since 1970 to try to change this situation?
3. Why has the UN had such little success in its attempts to change the situation?

B. Study the photograph above, then answer these questions:
1. What is 'apartheid'? What does the photograph reveal about apartheid?
2. Why might a critic of the UN claim that this was none of the ILO's business?
3. How might an ILO official reply to such critics?

Revision exercise

Test your understanding of words and terms to do with the UN by matching the items in column A with their correct definitions in column B.

A1 Charter

A2 Specialised Agencies

A3 World Bank

A4 Resolution 242

A5 Security Council

A6 Developing Nations Bloc

A7 Uniting for Peace

A8 New International Economic Order

A9 Veto

A10 Trust territories

B1 A 'bloc' in the General Assembly of 125 developing African, Asian, Caribbean and Latin American states.

B2 Former colonies governed by UN members until ready to govern themselves.

B3 A UN declaration in 1974 calling for the complete reorganisation of world trade, transport, industry, agriculture, money and technology.

B4 The right of permanent members of the Security Council to block any of its decisions by voting against it.

B5 A statement of the UN's principles and a list of the rules by which it is run.

B6 Independent, self-governing organisations, linked to the UN, dealing with social, economic and technical matters on an international level.

B7 A group of Specialised Agencies which provide UN members with development loans and currency reserves.

B8 A principal organ of the UN, responsible for maintaining international peace and security.

B9 Set of five UN proposals put forward in 1967 for a solution to the Arab–Israeli conflict.

B10 Procedure by which the General Assembly can take over the Security Council's peace-keeping functions if the Council's decisions are vetoed.

THE EUROPEAN COMMUNITY

'Here you are – don't lose it again.' A British cartoon of 1945

For over five hundred years, from the fifteenth to the twentieth centuries, Europe dominated the world. By 1939, when the Second World War began, European states had colonised over a third of the world's land surface. In doing so, they imposed European technology, law, methods of government and economic systems on half the human race.

As the power of the Europeans grew, so did their capacity to destroy. Over the centuries they fought many wars amongst themselves, each more destructive than the last. The Great War of 1914–18, which involved nearly all the major powers of Europe, killed more people than all previous wars put together.

Most Europeans said that the Great War must be a 'war to end all war', but the peace settlement they made in 1919 did not remove the causes of conflict.

Only twenty years later, a Second World War began.

The Second World War broke the power of Europe. At least 33 million Europeans were killed. Hundreds of their cities and towns were destroyed in air-raids, shellfire and street fighting. Between 50 and 60 million people were forced out of their homes – to be murdered in extermination camps, or to work as slave labour in foreign factories, or to become stateless, homeless refugees.

Part Three of this book tells a remarkable story. It is the story of how Europeans after the Second World War started to co-operate with each other to rebuild their shattered nations, eventually coming together in a 'European Community'. We will begin in 1945 by looking at the ruins on which this Community would be built.

13

EUROPE DESTROYED BY WAR

The Second World War of 1939–45 was the most destructive war in human history. Much of it was fought in Europe, and nearly every European state ended the war exhausted and broken. Sources A to H in this chapter give some idea of the terrible damage it caused.

A *The German city of Hamburg, photographed after its surrender to Allied forces on 3 May 1945*

Source B was written in 1949 by US Lieutenant-General Lucius Clay, one of the Allied military governors who ran Berlin after the defeat of Germany. It describes what he saw on arriving in Berlin in 1945.

B 'Wherever we looked we saw desolation. The streets were piled high with debris which left in many places only a narrow one-way passage between high mounds of rubble, and frequent detours had to be made where bridges and viaducts had been destroyed. . . The city was paralysed. Shortage of fuel had stopped the wheels of industry, Suffering and shock were visible in every face. Police and fire protection had broken down. Almost 3,000 breaks in the water mains were still to be repaired. Motor ambulances were not available and transport of the sick and dead was by handstretcher or by cart. Dead bodies still remained in canals and were being dug out from under bomb debris.'

Source C was written in 1985 by Martin Herz, a United States Army major during the War. It describes his memories of Vienna, capital of Austria, after its occupation by Soviet and American troops at the end of the war in 1945:

C 'The plain fact was that the Russian troops (which included a substantial proportion from Central Asia) had been allowed to go on a rampage of raping and looting when they occupied Vienna. . . I was for a while skeptical about the tales of 'tens of thousands' of raped women, but recall that a well-qualified doctor, who has to do with the approval of abortions requested by rape victims, explained to me that he had arrived at an estimate, which he regarded as conservative, of 70,000 cases of rape by Red Army soldiers. As for the looting, it was of two kinds – by soldiers going from house to house to take any objects of value or alcoholic spirits they could find, and the systematic removal by the occupation forces of machinery and equipment, some of it vital to the running of the city. . . Soviet soldiers sometimes slaughtered animals in houses and apartments; . . . the occupation troops seemed to take delight in relieving themselves on the furniture and carpets of 'capitalists'.

D *Refugees crossing the River Elbe in Germany in 1945 – just a few of an estimated 16 million Germans driven from their homes at the end of the war*

Source E was written in 1985 by an American soldier remembering his tour of duty in Greece in 1944–46.

E 'Athens [*in November 1944*] was definitely shabby. . . Hundred billion drachma notes . . . were the only currency in circulation. A wad of such bills about half and inch thick sufficed to buy a newspaper. There was remarkably little else for sale. Bushel baskets had long since replaced purses for carrying the all but worthless currency around, and individual bills drifted in the wind across the streets – too valueless for anyone to bother picking them up.'

Source F, dated 24 August 1945, comes from the diary of J. L. Hodson, a well-off and well-connected British journalist.

F 'The war is over; the conditions of war in some respects continue. . . I travelled last Sunday to Newcastle on Tyne. The journey which in peace-time took four hours now took eight and a quarter. No food on the train. No cup of tea to be got at the stops because the queues for this remarkable beverage masquerading as tea were impossibly long. At Newcastle an army artillery captain and I got hold of a truck and wheeled our bags along a platform almost impassable through luggage and merchandise waiting to be shifted. No taxi to be got. My hotel towel is about the size of a pocket handkerchief, the soap tablet worn to the thinness of paper, my bed sheets are torn.'

Source G is part of a news report by British journalist Robert Dunnett on BBC Radio's nightly 'War Report' on 3 May 1945.

G 'People in big Dutch towns have been keeping more and more to their houses. Some have on their doors notices saying 'Any food left here will be welcome', but they have not the strength to go out looking for it. Lacking coal for power and pumping they have no proper water supply. The death-rate is still increasing, and they are unable to bury the dead. Lacking wood they are making paper coffins and stacking them in churches. One man said that hardly any of the city children born in the last three years have survived.'

H European war deaths, 1939–45.

Belgium	28,031
Britain	244,723
Denmark	3,006
France	1,235,000
Germany	7,400,000
Greece	415,300
Italy	81,078
Netherlands	31,238
Norway	10,000
Poland	6,000,000
Portugal	–
Spain	–
Sweden	–
Yugoslavia	1,685,000

Work section

A. Using sources A to H as evidence, make a list of at least seven ways in which European countries in 1945 had been affected by the Second World War.

B. Study sources A and B.
   1. Describe how (a) a German civilian, and (b) a French civilian might have reacted to these scenes in 1945.
   2. Suggest how their feelings about such scenes might have affected the future relations between their countries.

C. Judging by sources A to H, how likely was it that Europeans in 1945 would want to co-operate with each other in future years? Explain your answer carefully.

EUROPE'S POSTWAR RECOVERY

From 1945 to 1950 the people of Europe made huge efforts to rebuild their shattered nations. In many cases, countries worked together towards recovery.

Relief and reconstruction

Even before the war was over, a United Nations Relief and Rehabilitation Administration (**UNRRA**) was created to help countries after they were freed from Axis occupation. Formed in 1943 by forty-four governments, UNRRA provided relief supplies such as food and clothing. It also helped rebuild damaged services such as transport and power supplies.

Similar bodies such as a European Coal Organisation and a UN Economic Co-operation Administration brought together many European governments in the work of reconstruction at the end of the war.

A United States of Europe?

Despite the efforts of such bodies, the damage to Europe could not be quickly repaired. The task, as you have seen, was very big. Winston Churchill, Britain's Prime Minister during the war, thought that wider co-operation between countries would be needed if Europe was to recover fully. In a speech at Zurich in Switzerland on 19 September 1946, Churchill said:

A '[The remedy] is to recreate the European fabric, or as much of it as we can, and to provide it with a structure under which it can dwell in peace, safety and freedom. We must build a kind of United States of Europe.'

Churchill's phrase 'a United States of Europe' quickly became a well-known slogan, and helped to spread the idea of European unity. Late in 1947 supporters of the idea formed an International Committee of the Movements for European Unity. In 1948 they organised a Congress of Europe, meeting at The Hague, which brought together 1,000 influential Europeans from twenty-six countries.

The main achievement of the Congress was the creation in 1949 of a **Council of Europe**. Consisting of ten western European states, the Council's function was to discuss matters of common interest and to work for the political and economic unity of Europe. However, it had no law-making powers and could not force member states to accept its decisions. Attempts to give the Council more power were blocked by Britain and the Scandinavian countries; they did not want to give up any of their own national power to a 'supra-national' body.

The OEEC

A more important and powerful body was the **Organisation for European Economic Co-operation (OEEC)**, set up in 1948.

The OEEC was created to deal with an economic crisis in 1947. Atrocious winter weather at the start of 1947 led to desperate fuel shortages across Europe. This was followed in the summer by the failure of many crops, forcing up food prices. Countries had to buy food and fuel from the United States, but soon used up their dollar reserves in doing so.

George Marshall, the US Secretary of State, declared that the US government would help European countries overcome their dollar shortage by giving them large-scale aid over the next few years. The European states would have to decide jointly how to spend this '**Marshall Aid**'.

Problems arose from this last point when talks about Marshall Aid began in Paris. The Soviet Foreign Minister, Molotov, protested that a joint aid programme would interfere in the internal affairs of countries. He argued that each country should decide for itself what aid it needed. The Soviet government therefore refused to accept Marshall Aid and put

The winning entry in a 1950 poster competition on the subject of Marshall Aid organised by the Economic Co-operation Administration

ALL OUR COLOURS TO THE MAST

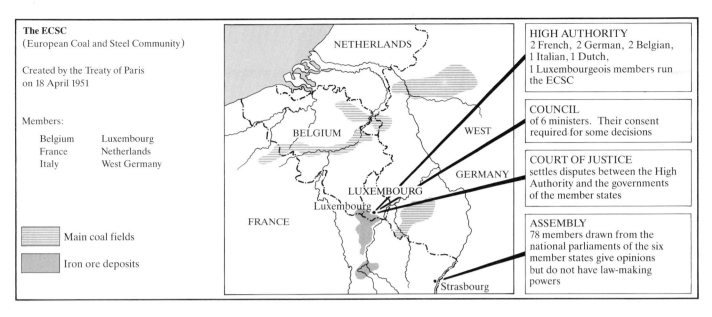

The ECSC
(European Coal and Steel Community)

Created by the Treaty of Paris
on 18 April 1951

Members:

Belgium   Luxembourg
France   Netherlands
Italy   West Germany

Main coal fields

Iron ore deposits

HIGH AUTHORITY
2 French, 2 German, 2 Belgian,
1 Italian, 1 Dutch,
1 Luxembourgeois members run
the ECSC

COUNCIL
of 6 ministers. Their consent
required for some decisions

COURT OF JUSTICE
settles disputes between the High
Authority and the governments
of the member states

ASSEMBLY
78 members drawn from the
national parliaments of the six
member states give opinions
but do not have law-making
powers

pressure on the countries of Eastern Europe, where it had great influence, to do the same.

As a result, only sixteen states accepted Marshall Aid, most of them in Western Europe. In April 1948 they formed the Organisation of European Economic Co-operation to decide what to do with it. Over the next four years the OEEC distributed $13,750,000,000 in aid to its members. It also did much to develop co-operation amongst them. For example, it set up a **European Payments Union** in 1950 to help countries trade more easily with each other by simplifying the rules for payment of goods.

The OEEC finished distributing Marshall Aid a year early, in 1951, but continued to work for European co-operation for the next ten years. It was replaced in 1961 by a similar body, the **Organisation for Economic Co-operation and Development**.

The Schuman Plan

On 9 May 1950 the French Foreign Minister, Robert Schuman, announced a new plan for European co-operation. The plan, whose details were drawn up by his colleague Jean Monnet, was to pool the coal and steel resources of France and Germany in an organis-ation which all European countries could join.

Schuman had two aims with his plan. The first was to bring France and Germany closer together and so reduce the chances of another war between them. The second was to set up an economic 'community', or grouping, as a first step towards European unity.

The Schuman Plan was different from any previous attempt at European unity. First, it did not try to unite countries in one move; instead, it aimed to cre-ate unity gradually by getting countries to work together on specific tasks. These tasks would be con-nected with the pooling of their basic industries – coal and steel. And second, this community would have common rules and organs, notably a High Authority, which would be independent of each member's government, but whose decisions would be binding on them. Schuman summed up his aims in these words:

B 'Five years, almost to the day, after Germany's unconditional surrender, France is taking the first decisive step in the reconstruction of Europe, and is associating Germany with it. . . . Europe will not be made all at once, or as a single whole . It will be built of concrete achievements which first create . . . solidarity.'

Six countries accepted the Schuman Plan – West Germany, France, Italy, Belgium, Luxembourg and the Netherlands. The union they created was called the **European Coal and Steel Community**. It was the first of several economic communities that would eventually lead to what people called 'The Common Market'.

Work section

A. Study the poster opposite then answer these questions:
1. What do (a) the ship's sails, (b) the ship's hull, and (c) the sea each represent?
2. Suggest what was putting the wind in the ship's sails.
3. What, in your opinion, was the overall message of the poster's artist?
4. Suggest why the Economic Co-operation Administration wanted a poster on this subject.

B. 1. Use your general knowledge to explain (or try to find out) how the British government differs from the government of the United States of America.
2. Judging by your answer to question 1, how would the British government have to change for there to be a 'United State of Europe'?
3. How did Schuman's view of European unity (Source B) differ from Churchill's view (Source A)?

15

THE ROAD TO ROME, 1950–57

Only months after Schuman announced his plan for pooling Europe's coal and steel, the French Prime Minister announced a plan for pooling Europe's military forces. The movement towards unity in Europe was gathering speed.

The European Defence Community

Since the end of the war in 1945, many states in western Europe had formed military alliances to protect themselves against possible attack by the Soviet Union.

By the **Brussels Treaty** of 1948, Britain, France, the Netherlands, Belgium and Luxemburg agreed to defend each other against any aggression in Europe, and to co-operate with each other in economic, social and cultural affairs.

In 1949 these five countries were joined by the USA, Canada, Portugal, Denmark, Ireland, Italy and Norway. Together they formed a **North Atlantic Treaty Organisation** (**NATO**), putting their defence forces under a joint command and agreeing that an attack on any one of them would be treated as an attack on them all.

In 1950 the outbreak of the Korean War (see Chapter 4) led the US government to demand the strengthening of NATO forces in Europe, in case the war should spread from the east. These forces would include some 150,000 German soldiers. The French refused to agree to this rebuilding of the German armed forces so soon after the Second World War. Instead the French Prime Minister, René Pleven, put forward his own proposals.

The Pleven Plan was for a Western European army, consisting of soldiers from each country, under a joint command. This would allow German soldiers to take part in Europe's defence without there being a new German army under German control. The Pleven Plan was accepted by the six countries which had formed the ECSC. In 1952 they agreed to form a **European Defence Community** (**EDC**), organised in the same way as the ECSC. Linked to it were plans for a European Political Community; there would be a common defence policy with a single defence minister, a Council of Ministers drawn from the member states, as well as a European Parliament.

These ambitious plans came to nothing, for the French parliament refused to agree to France joining the EDC. In its place a new body was created, the **Western European Union**. The WEU simply extended the 1948 Brussels Treaty by inviting West Germany and Italy to join it and to become members of NATO. As a balance to the armed forces that Germany would have to create to become a member, Britain agreed to keep four army divisions in Europe.

The Messina Conference, 1955

The failure of the EDC and of the proposed European Political Community showed how difficult it would be to unite Europe. As a result, pro-Europeans became less ambitious. When the Foreign Ministers of the six ECSC countries met at Messina in Italy in 1955 to discuss further steps towards unity, they made this declaration:

A '. . . the moment has arrived to initiate a new phase on the path of constructing Europe. . . This has to be done principally in the

Foreign Ministers of the 'Six' sign the Rome Treaties in 1957

economic sphere . . ., through an expansion of joint institutions, the gradual fusion of national economies, the creation of a common market, and the gradual coordination of social policies.'

Paul-Henri Spaak, Belgian Foreign Minister and a keen supporter of European unity, set up a committee to research how these aims could be achieved. The result was the Spaak Report of 1956, making proposals for a general union of countries and for union in the field of nuclear energy.

The Treaties of Rome, 1957

At further meetings in Italy in 1956, Foreign Ministers from the Six approved the Spaak Report and drew up plans for putting it into effect. Their plans resulted in the **Treaties of Rome** which they signed in 1957.

The Treaties of Rome created two new bodies, the European Economic Community (EEC) and the European Atomic Energy Commission (Euratom). Together with the ECSC they formed what people soon called **The Common Market**.

The main provisions of the Treaties of Rome were:
1. The removal of customs duties from goods passing between member states.
2. The creation of a uniform tariff (*a tax on trade*) on goods entering member states from non-members.
3. People should be free to move and settle within the Common Market.
4. Members should follow common policies towards agriculture and transport.
5. A European Social Fund would be set up to help areas suffering from social problems such as high unemployment or bad housing.
6. A European Investment Bank would give money to members to pay for major development projects.

EFTA

Britain did not sign the Treaties of Rome in 1958 and so did not become a founder member of the Common Market. There were three main reasons for this.

First, Britain feared that membership would result in a loss of sovereignty – that is, control of her own affairs. Second, much of Britain's trade was with Commonwealth countries such as New Zealand, and

'*Look what I made of the spare wheel*' – a cartoon in the Manchester Guardian *newspaper in June 1959 shows Britain's Trade Minister, Reginald Maudling, talking to President de Gaulle of France*

the British government feared this trade would be damaged if EEC tariffs were put onto imports from the Commonwealth. Third, Britain at that time was closely involved with the USA. The British government did not want to risk this 'special relationship' by getting too closely involved with Europe.

Nevertheless, Britain could see the advantages of free trade between European countries. Britain was also worried that Common Market tariffs would exclude it from valuable trade with the 'Six'. As a result, Britain in 1959 took the lead in setting up a **European Free Trade Area (EFTA)**, consisting of Austria, Britain, Denmark, Norway, Portugal, Sweden and Switzerland. These seven countries agreed to remove barriers to trade in manufactured goods between each other, but they kept their own tariffs on goods from outside EFTA.

For the 'outer seven', as the EFTA countries were known, this was a convenient arrangement. It gave them a useful degree of co-operation in trade, but did not involve them in the full political and economic co-operation required in the Common Market.

Work section

A. Look at the photograph opposite, then answer these questions using the information in this chapter:
1. Describe briefly what these men were agreeing to do.
2. Why would such an agreement have been impossible ten years earlier?
3. What had happened during those ten years to make this event possible?

B. Study the cartoon above, then answer these questions using information in this chapter.
1. Explain what each of the following mean: 'European Common Market', 'Inner 6', 'Outer 7', 'European Free Trade Area'.
2. How does the cartoonist suggest that the European Free Trade Area was inferior to the Common Market?
3. How might a supporter of the European Free Trade Area have portrayed it more favourably?

16

THE GROWTH OF THE EUROPEAN COMMUNITY

The Rome Treaties came into effect on 1 January 1958. The new **Common Market** made rapid progress. By 1961 it had reduced tariffs between its six members, devised a common external tariff, planned a Common Agricultural Policy (CAP), and was considering a political as well as economic union of the Six. Most noticeably, the Six were fast becoming richer than most other countries in Europe.

Britain, meanwhile, had run into economic problems. Having refused at first to join the Common Market, the British now saw it as a way out of their economic difficulties. Along with Ireland and Denmark, Britain therefore applied to become a member in 1961, hoping to share in its prosperity.

De Gaulle blocks Britain's entry

The British had left it too late. General de Gaulle, President of France, announced after long negotiations that he did not think Britain was ready to join the Common Market. The negotiations were promptly suspended. Some of de Gaulle's reasons for blocking Britain's entry can be seen in this extract from the press conference, in January 1963, at which he announced his objections:

A 'England is insular, maritime, linked by trade, markets and food supply to very different and often very distant lands. She is essentially an industrial and commercial nation, and her agriculture is relatively unimportant. . .

The question arises as to how far it is possible at the present time for Britain to accept a truly common tariff, as the Continent does, for this would involve giving up all Commonwealth preferences. . . Can she do this?

The entry, first, of Great Britain, and then of these (Free Trade Area) states will completely change the whole complex of . . . rules which have already been established between the Six. . . Then it will no longer be the same Common Market . . . but instead one with 11, or 13, or perhaps even 18 members which will have little resemblance to that built up by the Six. . . This Community, increasing in such fashion, would see itself faced with problems of economic relations with all kinds of other states, and first with the United States. . . Ultimately it would appear as a colossal Atlantic Community under American dependence and direction, and which would quickly have absorbed the Community of Europe.'

Four years later, in 1967, Britain made a second application to join the Common Market. Again, de Gaulle blocked the negotiations.

In 1969 de Gaulle resigned as President of France. His successor, Georges Pompidou assured the British Prime Minister, Edward Heath, that he would not oppose British entry. Negotiations were therefore re-started and Britain, along with Denmark and Ireland, joined the Common Market on 1 January 1973. The Six were now Nine.

The European Community

Meanwhile the Common Market continued to develop. In 1967 the three Common Market organisations – the EEC, Euratom and ECSC – merged into a single **European Community**. The Community was now run by a Council and a Commission based in Brussels, a Parliament in Strasbourg and a Court of Justice in Luxembourg. The diagram opposite shows how these bodies function.

In 1968 the customs union was completed. This meant that member states no longer had to pay each other customs duties when they traded goods. At the same time, a common external tariff for goods entering the Community was created.

B *'Joining the Club', drawn by the British cartoonist Vicky in 1963. Prime Minister Macmillan of Britain, dressed for cricket, asks to join the European football club. Chancellor Adenauer of Germany (centre) says to President de Gaulle of France 'He says he wants to join on his terms'.*

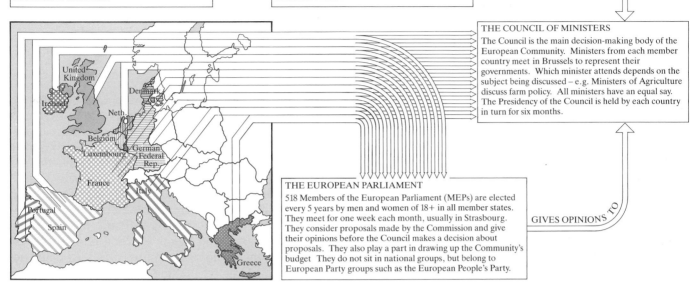

The European Community and its main institutions

THE COURT OF JUSTICE
The Court is composed of 13 judges, one from each member state. Its purpose is to give judgement on disputes arising from Community law. These might involve member states, companies, community institutions or individuals.

THE EUROPEAN COMMISSION
The Commission is the Civil Service of the European Community. It has 17 members, each responsible for one area of activity (e.g. agriculture, or the environment). The Commissioners are appointed by their governments. Their job is to make sure the Community is doing its work properly. They do this by proposing courses of action to the Council of Ministers.

MAKES PROPOSALS TO

THE COUNCIL OF MINISTERS
The Council is the main decision-making body of the European Community. Ministers from each member country meet in Brussels to represent their governments. Which minister attends depends on the subject being discussed – e.g. Ministers of Agriculture discuss farm policy. All ministers have an equal say. The Presidency of the Council is held by each country in turn for six months.

THE EUROPEAN PARLIAMENT
518 Members of the European Parliament (MEPs) are elected every 5 years by men and women of 18+ in all member states. They meet for one week each month, usually in Strasbourg. They consider proposals made by the Commission and give their opinions before the Council makes a decision about proposals. They also play a part in drawing up the Community's budget. They do not sit in national groups, but belong to European Party groups such as the European People's Party.

GIVES OPINIONS TO

In 1975, after the Six had become Nine, the European Community signed an agreement with forty-six former colonies in Africa, the Caribbean and the Pacific (ACP). The **Lomé Convention**, named after the capital of Togo where it was signed, gave the ACP countries virtually free access to the European Community for their products. It also guaranteed them stable earnings on the exports of thirty-six primary products, thus protecting them from sudden changes in world market prices.

The creation of a **European Monetary System (EMS)** in 1979 was a further step towards economic unity. In the EMS, the currencies of most member states were linked to each other by a European Currency Unit, the ECU. The basic aim was to establish set exchange rates so that the value of the currencies against each other could only rise or fall by small amounts. This was a further help to trade between members.

In January 1981 the Community was further enlarged when Greece joined it. In January 1986 Portugal and Spain also joined, raising the number of member states to twelve.

Finally, in 1987, a new treaty known as the **Single Act** prepared the Community for a new phase of development in 1992. In that year the Twelve nations would become a single market of 320 million people. The frontiers dividing them would disappear, and there would be complete freedom of movement throughout the Community. Common commercial laws would make it attractive to form European companies and joint ventures.

Work section

A. Study sources A and B, then answer these questions:
1. In source B, who had drawn up the rules of the European 'club' that Macmillan wanted to join?
2. Find at least three reasons in source A why de Gaulle blocked Britain's entry to the 'club'.
3. What other reasons are shown in source B for de Gaulle's opposition to British entry?
4. Is it possible to tell from source B whether the cartoonist agreed or disagreed with de Gaulle's reasons for blocking Britain's entry?

B. Study the diagram above, then fit the descriptions in column A to the names which match them in column B:

A1 Main decision-making body of the European Community	B1	Brussels
A2 HQ of the Council of Ministers, Commission and most committees of Parliament	B2	Council of Ministers
	B3	MEPs
A3 Body which makes proposals for Community laws, makes sure members abide by the Rome Treaties, and administers common policies	B4	Strasbourg
	B5	Court of Justice
	B6	European Commission
A4 Body which judges disputes arising from Community law	B7	Luxembourg
A5 Meeting place of the European Parliament	B8	President of the Council

17

ACHIEVEMENTS AND PROBLEMS OF THE EUROPEAN COMMUNITY

By 1990 the European Community was a well-established part of the world scene. It was possible to look back over its thirty-three-year life and assess what it had and had not achieved.

The CAP

Some of the EC's best achievements as well as its greatest problems came from its **Common Agricultural Policy (CAP).**

Introduced during the 1960s, the CAP had two basic aims. The first was to ensure that everyone in the EC had enough to eat at affordable prices. The second was to guarantee a reasonable income to the Community's millions of farmers.

The CAP tries to achieve these aims by controlling the price of farm produce. Each year the Council of Ministers sets **target prices** for produce such as fruit, grain, wine, milk, eggs and beef. This target price is the money that a farmer could reasonably expect to get at market for his produce. If the market price falls below the target price, the EC intervenes by buying his produce at a higher price. This **intervention price** is meant to make sure that farmers have a guaranteed income, even when their produce is difficult to sell.

In some ways the CAP has worked well. Farm output and farmers' incomes have risen sharply since the 1960s. This has helped poor rural areas of the EC to prosper. It has also meant that most people in the EC can take it for granted that their shops are always stocked with reasonably priced food.

A 'mountain' of skimmed milk powder purchased by the CAP, photographed in 1982

On the other hand, the CAP has allowed farmers to produce far more food than the Community needs. Production of milk, wine, meat and grain rocketed in the 1970s and 1980s because farmers knew the EC would buy them even if they could not sell them at market. This led to the creation of huge food reserves, held in gigantic warehouses until they could be sold. All to often it proved difficult to get rid of these 'mountains' and 'lakes' of food and drink, except by selling them at very low prices to countries outside the EC or by making them into animal feed. The CAP came in for much hostile criticism for this.

Financial problems

With the CAP costing £12.5 billion a year out of a total EC budget of £17.5 billion, member states looked, in the 1980s, for ways to reform both the CAP and the budget. The British especially looked for changes. In 1980 the British Government complained that its contribution of £1,180 million to the budget was unfairly high in comparison to the contributions of other members. Germany, for example, the richest member paid £699 million. Britain's demand for a refund of £1 billion caused long and angry arguments with the rest of the Community.

Even after Britain was given a refund of £1.5 billion over two years, arguments about Community finance continued. Although there was a danger that the EC would go bankrupt without financial reform, the British government blocked any increase in spending on the CAP until its contributions to the EC budget had been reduced still further.

At the same time, in the 1980s, the European Parliament began to use its power to veto the EC's annual budget. Angered by the failure of the Council of Ministers to reform the CAP, it vetoed the budget in 1980 and 1984, causing financial chaos.

The EC was thus caught between two extremes – the urgent need to reform its finances, and the equally urgent demand of the British government for a reduction in its contribution to the finances.

Crisis in the ACP states

The 1975 Lomé Convention between the European Community and the African, Caribbean and Pacific states (see page 37) seemed at first to be one of the Community's major achievements.

Renewed in 1981 and 1985, and expanding to include sixty-six ACP countries, the Lomé Convention

British people demonstrate against membership of the European Community in 1975

helped these mostly poor states by letting them trade freely with the EC and by stabilising their export earnings. The Lomé Convention also gave them aid which helped to build 10,000 km of roads, 25 major water schemes, 53 hospitals with 4,200 beds and 372 schools for 86,000 students.

Many of these benefits, however, were wiped out in the 1980s by a world recession, spiralling debt and high interest rates. Far from growing richer through their links with the EC, many ACP states faced the prospect of acute poverty in the 1990s.

Regional development

Parts of the European Community are very wealthy. Others are very poor. Hamburg in northern Germany, for example, is five times richer than Thrace in north-eastern Greece. The Scottish Highlands and Islands are poor in comparison with south-east England.

To offset such regional differences, the EC created a **Regional Development Fund** in 1975. Between 1975 and 1985 more than £8 billion was put into 29,000 development projects in the poorer regions of the EC. These projects included the building of roads, telecommunications, ports and water supplies. Money was also given for job-creating investments in industry.

Despite such spending, the Regional Development Fund did not seem to have much impact on the poorest regions of Europe. Average incomes in western Ireland and Southern Italy, for example, were only a fifth of those in places like Paris, London and Brussels. The Fund was therefore reformed in

1984 so that most aid was given to the very poorest regions instead of spreading it over all the poor areas.

The sovereignty issue

As the EC approached 1992, when the Single European Act was due to remove all remaining barriers to trade between members, arguments continued over what sort of Community it should become. Should it be a United States of Europe, with a single government for all member states, a common currency and laws? Or should it be a collection of independent states, each retaining sovereignty – that is, control over its own affairs? The British Prime Minister, Margaret Thatcher, summarised one side of the argument in a radio interview in 1988:

A 'It is not possible to have a United States of Europe. What is possible is for the twelve countries of Europe to . . . trade more closely and have fewer formalities across borders – but not to dissolve our own infinite variety, our own nationality, our own identity. I think Europe will be stronger because it has Britain in as Britain, France in as France, Spain in as Spain. I do not wish them to dissolve into some common sort of neutral personality.'

But whatever the future of the Community, and whatever problems it had yet to overcome, the EC had at least achieved one of the basic aims of its founders. After centuries of warfare between the states of Western Europe, culminating in two world wars in the twentieth century, war between any of them seemed completely unlikely.

Work section

A. Study the photograph opposite, then answer these questions:
1. Describe in your own words the Common Agricultural Policy of the European Community.
2. Using your knowledge of the CAP, explain how this 'mountain' of milk powder was created.
3. How might (a) an opponent of the CAP and (b) a farmer in the EC react to this scene?

B. Study the photograph above, then answer these questions:
1. Judging by the photograph, as well as by the information in this chapter, explain why some British people wanted to leave the European Community in 1975.
2. How might a supporter of the EC have argued against their point of view?

Revision exercise

Divide a page into four columns, as shown in the example below.

Then, after completing the items in the list of *Steps towards European Unity*, put them into the appropriate columns in chronological order.

Finally, answer the questions beneath.

Steps towards European Unity, 1945–1990

United Nations R. . . . . and R. . . . . Administration (UNRRA), 1943
International C. . . . . . . of the Movements for European Unity, 1947
Organisation for European Economic C. . . . . (OEEC), 1948
The Brussels T. . . . ., 1948
The Council of E. . . . ., 1949
The North A. . . . . . Treaty Organisation (NATO), 1949
European P. . . . . . Union (EPU), 1950
The Schuman P. . ., 1950
European Coal and S. . . . Community (ECSC), 1952
European Defence C. . . . . . . (EDC), 1952
European P. . . . . . . Community (EPC), 1952
W. . . . . . European Union (WEU), 1954
European E. . . . . . Community (EEC), 1958
European Atomic E. . . . . Authority (Euratom), 1958
European Free T. . . . Association (EFTA), 1959
The European C. . . . . (EC: a merger of the EEC, ECSC and Euratom), 1967
The EC grows from six to n. . . member states, 1973
The Lomé Convention, 19. .
The EC grows to t. . member states, 1981
The EC grows to twelve member states, 19. .
The S. . . . . European Act, 1987

Example:

Year	Economic	Political	Military
1943	United Nations Relief and Rehabilitation Administration		
1947		International Committee of the Movements for European Unity	

1. Judging by your completed table, in which of the three areas has European unity been most successful?
2. In which period of time were the most important steps towards unity taken? How do you explain this?
3. In which column do you think events are most likely to take place in the next ten years? Explain your answer.